THESE BROKEN ROADS

From the outset of *These Broken Roads*, author Donna Hayes finds herself asking, "How did I get here?" The answer is a doozy. A corporate executive at an international investment bank in New York City, Hayes arrived by way of a small town in Jamaica where she grew up among chickens, superstitions, and grief at having been abandoned by both of her parents. In her teens, Hayes' mother returns to bring her into an unfamiliar family in America where she continues her quest for safety and love.

These Broken Roads is Hayes' Cinderella story, beginning in the Jamaican countryside and ending in an Uptown penthouse. It is a journey from betrayal to self-discovery. It is a coming of age that is at once human and hopeful. Hayes' life, though complicated by duplicity, is consistently buoyed by a strength and competence that is in moments, breathtaking. Pick up this book. You will not be able to put it down.

—Joselin Linder, author of *The Family Gene*, HarperCollins

· · · ·

Although Donna Hayes' first book, *These Broken Roads*, is the story of the empowering and indomitable feminine spirit, it is not a feminist book. It is a story of a woman that faces seemingly insurmountable odds not just to survive but to flourish and thrive. Magical, painful, cathartic, and thrilling at once.

—Thomas G. Waites, actor, teacher, and filmmaker

A glorious testament to the triumphant spirit we all have within. Donna shares her remarkable life story with incredible vulnerability and clarity. Taking us on a journey from rural Jamaica to the high rises of the Upper East side of Manhattan, filled with challenges that are ultimately turned into lessons....for us all. Bravo, a beautiful read.

—Annie McGovern, actor, director/producer, singer, and VP of Simulations, Inc.

. . . .

A riveting memoir, *These Broken Roads* is an against all odds story, told with brazen honesty by Donna Hayes, a woman whose childhood abandonment leads her down a path driven by a desperate need for love, only to find herself in abusive relationships with three damaged men. Ultimately, she finds the strength she needs to leave her troubled past behind and begin the healing process through her enduring power of faith.

—Robin Bobbé, Modernager Casting, owner

. . . .

There are so many levels to enjoy and learn from in Donna Hayes' amazing new book. There is a vivid depiction of the sights and sounds of Hayes' both difficult and joyous Jamaican upbringing as well as the twists and turns of a young woman struggling to find success and romance far from home. The disappointments she experiences and then her eventual triumph both professionally and romantically add to the compelling and wonderful read that is Hayes' memoir."

—Ellen Sherman, Writer, Producer and host of the Binge or Bomb podcast

THESE BROKEN ROADS

Scammed and Vindicated
One Woman's Story

DONNA MARIE HAYES

Sibylline Press

AN IMPRINT OF ALL THINGS BOOK

Sibylline Press
Copyright © 2023 Donna Marie Hayes
All Rights Reserved.

Published in the United States by Sibylline Press,
an imprint of All Things Book LLC, California.
Sibylline Press is dedicated to publishing the brilliant work of
women authors ages 50 and older.
www.sibyllinepress.com

Distributed to the trade by Publishers Group West.
Sibylline Press
Paperback ISBN: 978-1-7367954- 4-6
eBook ISBN: 978-1-960573-04-9
Library of Congress Control Number: 2023935598

Book and Cover Design: Alicia Feltman
Cover photo courtesy of Dorothy Shi, Dorothy Shi Photography
www.dorothyshiphotography.com

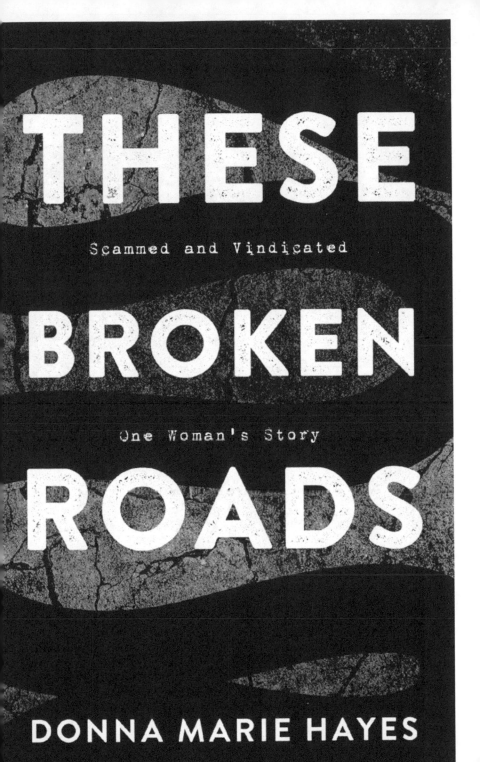

THESE

Scammed and Vindicated

BROKEN

One Woman's Story

ROADS

DONNA MARIE HAYES

Dedication

This book is dedicated to all the little girls who suffer in silence, swirling around in feelings of inadequacy and unworthiness, yearning for scraps of attention and emotional nourishment. You may not hear this often, but you are a beautiful and unique being and matter so much more than you realize. Always have and always will be.

Some names have been changed for privacy protection.

You are not the darkness you endured.
You are the light that refused to surrender.

– John Mark Green

One

OUR TIME

IT HAS BEEN TWO WEEKS since Javier De Leon downloaded the Our Time app on his iPhone. He sits at his mother's kitchen table in her Grand Concourse apartment in the Bronx, New York, and scrolls through the dating profiles of middle-aged widows and divorcées. He studies their shiny profiles and faces.

Too serious. Swipes left.
Too muscular. Swipes left.
Too slutty. Swipes left.
Too much make-up. Swipes left.
Too plain. Swipes left.

A smile creeps across his face as my picture fills his screen. He studies my profile.

"Moonlights as an actress and singer. Loves God, dogs and helping the helpless. Not looking for a one-night stand. Works as a corporate executive for an international investment bank."

He leans against the plastic-covered dining room chair and swipes right.

"Hi there, New York Dee," he whispers to no one in particular.

* * *

I am curled up on my brand-new olive-green couch in my Upper East Side Manhattan rental. I admire my new space, freshly decorated with accent pieces of burnt orange and pink. An oversized fluffy white rug sits in the middle of the room beneath a small glass table. I love this apartment. It's expensive, but I feel safe here, especially after two failed marriages—the last one ended with me literally running for my life. A canned message appears on my screen.

"I like your profile. I would love to hear from you."

He doesn't really expect to hear from me, but I like his caramel-colored face and profile.

He is a divorced father who loves to cook, hike, dance and take care of his two boys. He considers himself to be a spiritual person who loves sunsets and God. I study his brown eyes and find myself wondering if he is as kind as they look.

It has been eight years since my divorce and a relationship.

I write back within the hour, and we meet at a Thai restaurant on the Upper West Side a week later. This is how I imagine that things were set in motion.

Two

BIG PEOPLE BUSINESS

1967

I PULL BACK THE CURTAINS, and a sliver of moonlight spills across the settee. My five-year-old mind is working overtime as I study her large, shadowy silhouette, which is outlined in the darkness across the yard. I tiptoe to the window on the other side of the house and peer into the darkness. My grandparents, who I call Mama and Dada, although they are neither, are talking in the kitchen, which is separate from the living quarters, where light from the kerosene lamp casts large, duppy shadows across the wall. I hurry back to the front door and turn the lock as quietly as I can and slip out into the swirling darkness. A light, soft wind rustles the trees and blows through my pajamas. My tiny body shivers as I hurry toward the tall ghostlike-looking tree, my bare feet make a crunching sound atop the gravel.

The cow's large black liquid eyes gaze down at me in the shadows as I brush my tiny hands against her large body. I try to remove the knotted nylon rope from around her neck, but it's too tight. It hurts my hands. Tears of frustration form at the corner of my eyes and melt down my face. I plop down at the base of the trunk of the tree, her hot breath raining down on my face. I look up at the sky. The stars look like a million twinkling fireflies. I ask God to help the cow.

"You are a very nice cow. It is going to hurt just a little bit, but you are going to cow heaven, and you are going to be very happy," I whisper and cry in her soft fur, before hurrying up the veranda stairs, through the living room and back in bed. I am still sobbing as I settle under the covers.

The next morning, I watch from the corner of the red veranda with eyes as wide as saucers as the bad butcher men push and pull and stab and cut.

I hate those big ugly stupid butcher men.

I look over at the pasture where the herd of cows is grazing and swishing their long tails. I see the cow's baby calf among them. I feel sorry for him, because he doesn't have a mommy anymore. Just like me. Except my mother isn't dead, she is alive and well in Kingston but left me here in the country to live with her mother, Mama.

The sound of my grandmother's voice pulls me back. "Donna!"

"Yes, Mama? Coming, Mama."

I make my way to the tiny makeshift kitchen across the yard. Her humming and the smell of curry fill the air. Our dogs, Jane Grip and Lion, eye me lazily from beneath the shade of the small berry tree as I enter the kitchen.

"Go bring me some water," she orders without looking up from all the meat that she hacks at.

"Yes, Mama." I mosey to the front of the house and scoop some water out of the large rusty drum pan with the white plastic pail. The bad butcher men and Dada are wrapping pieces of meat in thick plastic and putting them in metal pans. I roll my eyes at them.

I place the bucket on the long wooden table and plop down on the small stool in the corner to watch Mama. My grandmother is short and thin with flawless skin that reminds me of dark chocolate. She hinges her jaw forward, clicks her false teeth together and hums "Jesus Keeps Me Near the Cross." This is how I know she is in deep concentration. My eyes follow her swift movements as she chops vegetables and sprinkles seasonings on the chunks of meat before lowering them in a large silver frying pan. Thick pieces of yellow yams, green bananas and dasheen are placed in a second pot which is bubbling wildly with hot water.

"Mama?"

"Hmmm?" She kneads flour and cornmeal in a separate bowl and continues humming. "Do you think the cow went to heaven?"

"Only the good Lord knows." Mama drops a sprig of thyme in the pot with the hand that is covered with the white-and-yellow mixture.

"Is her calf baby sad that he doesn't have a mother anymore?"

"A cow!" She glances at me with a chuckle. "God put the animals here for us to eat. If we nuh eat, we dead." She returns to kneading.

Silence hangs. I stare out the window and watch the leaves on the ackee tree bending gently under the pressure of a soft breeze. I choose my words carefully.

"Mama, how come my mother didn't keep me in Kingston with her when I was a baby?"

"Jesus, pickney! Me tell you already. She have to work, and she need somebody to take care of you." She sighs before dropping a disc-shaped dumpling in the second pot.

"She came for Grace when she was five, so how come she can't come for me?"

"Yuh ah police with all yuh questions?" Mama glances at

me with a slight grin and wipes the sweat from her face with the back of her hand.

"I am five years old now. Why can't she come for me now?"

"Jesus Savior, pilot me! Stop asking me foolishness. You nuh see me a cook?" She turns to face me with a flash of annoyance in her eyes.

"But I want to live with my own mother, and I feel sad like the calf baby." I play with the hem of my dress and fight tears. I don't want her to give me something to cry for. I can feel her eyes on me.

"You haunted? Come out of the kitchen and stay out of big people business." Mama's voice is impatient as she waves me away before turning back to the large steaming pots.

Whenever she doesn't want to tell me something, she calls it big people business. I hate when she does that, but I can't say anything, or I will get the leather strap. I shuffle across the yard, through our bedroom and into the extra room.

I gaze up at the two pictures that hang high on the wall above me. My mother is short and plump. She sits on a winged armchair, legs crossed at the ankles with her fingers intertwined over both knees. Her yellow-patterned dress is bold against her dark skin and her smile beams. I try to remember being near her as a baby.

How did she smell?

Did she hold me up in the air and smile at me?

Did she tell me that she loves me? Does she miss me?

My father's picture is in a brown wooden frame diagonal to my mother's. He stands erect. His young handsome face is thin and angular. He is dressed in a Jamaican police uniform, white shirt and black pants with shiny red banding around the waist that also extends down the side of each leg. A black oversized peaked cap sits atop his head, shadowing his serious face.

I fall to my knees under the pictures. With my small hands clasped below my chin, I pray to the people who left me here. People I don't really remember. I introduce myself and "tell" them about my life with Mama and Dada. We don't have running water like the Adrian family who live at the bottom of the hill, so I carry water from the standing pipe and fill the drum pans at the front of the house. I can even balance the bucket on my head with a cotta. I will go to Duncans Primary School next year, and I am going to do what Mama says and get good book learning. I help Dada to feed the pigs, goats and chickens.

Sometimes I help him to milk the cows and goats. Sweeping the yard with the straw broom is not my favorite, but I do it without Mama having to tell me to. I bathe myself good in the large metal washtub that Mama uses to wash the clothes before hanging them to dry on the line, and I always say my grace before I eat and my night prayers.

"Please may I come and live with you? I promise to be a good girl. Thank you. Amen." I whisper.

"Donna, come eat," Mama calls from the kitchen later that evening.

"Coming, Mama." I quickly head back to the kitchen.

Dada is leaning against the door with his arms folded, talking to Mama. Dada is her husband but not my real grandfather. I like him. But not on the Saturdays that he kills the poor animals.

"Dada. Why oonu have to kill the cow?" The words escape before I can stop them. I look up at his tall dark frame. My question amuses him. He throws his head back and laughs until I can see the pink at the roof of his mouth.

"Because we have to eat. Me tell yuh already!" Mama interrupts before he can answer.

He smiles awkwardly at me and removes his work boots. "I have a piece of sweetie in my pocket for you, if you eat all your supper." Dada pats his pocket with a sly smile.

"You betta eat all yuh supper first!" Mama interrupts again and places a plate of oxtails, gungo peas and rice with fried plantains in front of me.

"Yes, Mama."

I hide the oxtails on the side of my chair and toss them to the dogs, Lion and Jane Grip, when Mama isn't looking. I will not eat my cow friend!

Later that night, Mama pulls back the covers on the bed that I share with her and Dada. I don't sleep in the extra room because the shadows on the walls look like twisted wild duppies. I say the Lord's Prayer before snuggling into sheets that smell like carbolic soap.

"Go sleep," Mama commands before walking between the floral doorway curtains to join Dada. Probably to drink Milo, the sweet hot chocolate drink they like to sip on every night before bed.

"Yes, Ma'am." The flickering light from the kerosene lamp creates a yellow circular shadow in one corner of the ceiling. I glance sleepily in the direction of the extra room where the pictures of my parents hang high on the wall, in the darkness. I fall asleep, lost in a colorful fantasy of my mother.

We walk hand in hand along the street of a beautiful, shiny city wearing bright red dresses and sparkly shoes. I listen to the click-clacking sound of our polished heels against the perfumed pavement. I look up at my mother's smiling radiant face. Music swells and she takes my small hand in hers. We sway to the music like satin ribbons on a breezy afternoon. Twisting. Twirling. She lifts and holds me against her as sleep takes me.

Dada works at a factory, but I am not sure where. Each morning he puts on the clothes that Mama washes, starches and irons until they are as stiff as wood. Then he slips on his big shiny boots that he keeps under the bed. Mama gives him coffee with hard-dough bread and butter and then he walks down to the main road and disappears around the bend. He never comes back before dark. Mama spends the days cooking, cleaning and ironing. Some days she goes away for a while. On those days, I feel as if I am the only person in the universe. I sit under the two pictures and talk to my Mommy and Daddy, shuffle about the yard, play jacks on the veranda or chase the dogs around the house. Sometimes I eat the mangos and naseberries that fall from the trees until I have a bellyache.

I am singing Neil Diamond's "Sweet Caroline" at the top of my lungs to the chickens, the two lazy dogs and the colorful flowers at the side of the house. I imagine that they are clapping. I bow. They clap louder. I take another bow. From the corner of my eye, I notice Miss Daisy, the crazy lady who lives across the street, watching me from her yard. The fear washes over me as I hurry up the steps of the red veranda. I settle in a corner and watch her as she moves aimlessly about her yard, which is directly across the narrow-graveled path from our house. People say that she is a crazy madwoman. She climbs upon a large rock at the back of her house and says a lot of bad words. A lot. She stops only to start a new series of cursing and high-pitched screams. I study her small frame and her hair, which is a wild tangled wispy mop of gray. She shuffles down the dirt path toward the cemetery.

I tip-toe toward the gate so that I can see her through the clearing. She stomps into the cemetery and stretches her body across the tombstones and pounds on them furiously, while filling the hot air with her screams and cussing.

"Mama, what happened to Miss Daisy? This morning she was saying a lot of bad words."

Mama looks up from the large silver wash basin that she is washing the sheets in. "Dat woman deh mad! Don't go to her house if she calls you. You hear me, pickney?" Mama holds my gaze and a soapy finger near my face. Her voice is serious.

"Yes, Mama." I want to tell her that Miss Daisy scares me, and I want to go and live with my mother, but I keep quiet and watch her work. She does strange things to our clothes. She dips them in a blue liquid, beats them against a rock, scrubs them against a metal washboard, then hangs them on the line.

"Mama, I want to write a letter to my mother." I study her face and hand her a clothespin as she drapes a large white sheet over the clothesline.

"Oh, yeah?" She takes two clothespins and clips both end of the sheet that is blowing wildly in the wind. "Well, I never get no book learning, so you have to go ask Miss Ginny to help you write it." She clips one end of Dada's pants to the line. "Take some paper down to Miss Ginny and ask her to spell the words for you."

"Can I go now, Mama?" I feel the excitement filling me up. "Gwaan."

My five-year-old legs can't move fast enough as I hurry down the steep hill, past the cemetery and onto the main road until I get to Mama's friend's house and push the large iron gate open. Miss Ginny sits on her veranda, rocking in her chair. She seems to always be in the same spot. Rocking. Looking straight ahead. She doesn't say much, and I have never seen her smile. She makes me a little nervous, but I need to get a letter to my mother.

"Good afternoon, Miss Ginny."

"Yes?" She looks straight ahead. Rocking.

"Mama send me to ask you if you can help me write a letter to my mother. I have paper." I raise the white-lined paper up in the air for her to see. She stares straight ahead. Awkwardness fills the silence. I look down at my feet. Finally, she stands and enters her house. In a few minutes she returns with a book for me to press against and a pencil. I sit on the cool tile of her veranda, and she spells out each word until I have a letter to my mother.

December 1967

To Miss Mavis Green. Greetings. Thank you for the Christmas card. I saw your picture; it is very nice. I am your daughter Donna Pinnock from Duncans. I hope to see you some day. I hope you are well. As it leaves me nothing more to say.

Till I hear from you again.
– Donna Pinnock

This will remind her that I am still here, and she will come for me. Mama mails it and I wait.

Three

BROWN GIRL IN A RING

MAMA WALKS ME TO SCHOOL on my first day. It is a very long walk and my hands are tired from holding my bag with my pencils, erasers, crayons and notebook, but I am so excited to finally go to Duncans Primary School that I don't mind. I can't wipe the grin off my face. I look down again and again at my canary-colored shirt and blue uniform that has been starched and pressed to perfection. Last night I watched Mama dunk it in starch and iron it pleat by pleat until it is stiff as a rock. My socks are neatly rolled down to meet my new shiny black shoes that glisten in the sun. I can hear the school bell ringing as we walk along the dirt road.

"Mek sure you listen to the teacher and get your book learning. You hear me?" She points her finger at me, her face wrinkled with seriousness.

"Yes, Mama."

We all line up in front of a large door. When the teacher gives us the cue, we walk in a neat single file to our class and sing church songs.

There are a lot of rules. They don't tolerate any slackness. One of the most important ones is being on time. We are not allowed to be late unless we have a very good excuse. If your excuse is foolishness, the teacher will strike you several times in the palm of your hand with a leather strap. But if you do something really bad, you will get lashes on your back.

Within a few months, I am settled into my new school routine. In the mornings, I do my chores of collecting eggs, feeding the goats and pigs, and have my breakfast before starting the walk to school. Lunchtime, I make my way home for hard-dough bread or boiled banana and yellow yam covered with coconut oil. The drink is always brown sugar with water. In the evenings, I do my homework on the red veranda with Lion and Jane Grip looking on, and then a big supper before bed.

I like school because I get to play with other children instead of just lazy Lion and Jane Grip. The bell rings, heralding recess, my favorite part of the day. We all pour into the schoolyard. The boys usually play cricket. The girls play hopscotch, ring games or "hot pepper," a rope-skipping game where you have to jump really, really, really fast. If the rope hits your leg, it burns like hot pepper.

"Oonu want to play *Brown Girl in a Ring?*" One of my classmates asks excitedly.

Without hesitation we hold hands, form a circle and begin to sing.

"Who's first?" she yells out as we start singing.

There's a brown girl in a ring, Tra-la-la-la-lah.

My best friend Naomi jumps into the middle and saunters along the inside of the circle. We sing louder.

There's a brown girl in a ring, Tra-la-la-la-lah.

We hop up and down like excited rabbits as she skips around the circle, her long braids flapping in the warm air. Our faces flood with laughter.

Show me your motion, Tra-la-la-la-lah.

With arms akimbo, she dances and wiggles her waist and thrusts her hips forward. We throw our heads back with giggles.

Show me your partner, Tra-la-la-la-lah.

She points at me. According to the rules of the game, the person pointed to must join the person in the middle of the circle to dance. I release someone's hand and step toward the middle of the circle. We are singing at the top of our little lungs. I place my hands on my waist and face Naomi. We are dancing and laughing under the hot sun.

A tall boy jumps above us and punts a ball back to his friends who are shouting and chasing him. "Catch it. Catch it. Catch—"

His hard body slams into me and I stumble backward. Flailing. Trying to reach for something. Anything. The back of my head collides with something hard and sharp. I think it's a rock. Everything is a hazy blur except for random, colorful flashes. There is a circle around me. I try to look at their faces, but their images come and go. Pain throbs violently around my skull and I am pretty sure it has cracked opened. I try to move. Someone tells me not to. A sickening flow of warm fluid is pooling around my neck. Then everything slows down. I gaze at the sunlight peeking through the branches. The sky is fuzzy and blue. Then nothing.

Someone is picking me up. I am floating through a dark, empty space. I can hear car horns and voices as I soar higher and higher. I think I hear Mama's voice. I try to say her name, but my voice doesn't work anymore.

I slowly open my eyes and immediately close them. The bright light that fills wherever I am hurts my brain.

"She wake up! She wake up!" Mama's voice is too loud. I think I am lying across her lap. I smell curry. "Donna. Donna. You hear me? Thank the good Lord Jesus. Praise the Lord."

"Yes. Ma...ma."

"Donna. Can you open your eyes?"

I recognize Dr. Foote's voice. He lives in the big house across from his office. He has a big scary dog that chases me sometimes. I don't like Dr. Foote's big black ugly dog. I think I will tell him. Someone is prying my eyes open. I see the fuzzy grainy image of Dr. Foote, behind a bright light that he is shining into one eye. Then the other eye. I want to tell him about his ugly dog, but I can't keep my eyes open. Mama sits me up and the room is upside down. The back of my head is hammering, and I reach up to touch it. My hand is greeted by a thick bandage that the doctor orders me not to touch. I don't remember coming to the doctor. I only remember the big boy knocking me down.

Where did Mama come from?

"She must stay in bed." I listen to Dr. Foote talking to Mama. "Watch her carefully and take her to Falmouth Hospital if she gets worse."

"Yes, Doctor. God bless you, Doctor." Mama's voice sounds thick and heavy as if she is under water.

Someone picks me up. A car is humming. When did it get dark?

I sleep for two days. On the third day, I sit up in bed and Mama changes the bandage. My head still hurts, but it no longer feels as if someone's hand is inside my head squeezing as hard as possible. Mama feeds me some cerasee tea. Then later on, some soup. Later still, she comes back with some nasty-smelling bush tea. I turn my head.

"Drink it. It's for your own good." She gives me the look that I know too well. Every month, I am given a "wash out," which is a horrible-tasting concoction of herb bushes or Sinkle Bible (aloe vera). One day I refused to drink it. Mama and Dada held me down and placed a stick across my mouth and poured it down my throat. The same way they give the calves medicine. I cried that day until I was pretty sure I had no more tears.

"It's for your own good." Mama wiped my tears and handed me an orange. I sat on the veranda all day, mad that they treated me like an old cow.

I swallow the nasty drink in two gulps and hand the cup to Mama before settling back on the pillow.

"There is a God up in heaven who have his hand on your life. You know dat. Right?"

"Yes, Ma'am," I lie. I don't even know what that means. All I know is what I heard when Mama was talking to Dr. Foote. My head cracked open, I had something he called a concussion. It is serious enough that I have to stay in bed for two weeks. I don't even have to do chores. I like that.

"Dr. Foote said that with all that bleeding you should a dead. Remember that God save you for a reason. No matter what happen to you in life, never forget this day. You are a special child. If me don't know nutting else, that me know!"

"Yes, Mama." Whatever that means.

Four

SHERLOCK HOLMES

1970

IT IS A FRIDAY EVENING and dusk is falling as I make my way up the hill toward our house. Dada and a strange man are standing on the veranda. I lift the latch from the rusty iron gate and walk toward them.

"Good afternoon, Dada. Good afternoon, Sir." Dada is never home this early.

They say weak hellos and resume their hushed conversation. I hurry past them and across the yard to the kitchen. The smell of cassava pudding hangs in the air.

"Good afternoon, Mama. Who is that man with Dada?"

"Go take off your uniform and come help me do something." She ignores my question and chops at a large bunch of callaloo that litters the wooden table that is already covered with flour and sugar.

Big people business.

I do as I am told, and then hurry back to Mama.

"Yes, Mama?" I look around the room, searching for a clue to why Mama and Dada are acting so strange.

"Go into the living room and tell me what you see?"

"Wha...?"

"Just go and look, pickney!" she barks.

I enter the living room and am swollen with confusion and curiosity. My eyes wander to the floral settee, then over to the brown and gold dining room set that is as heavy as iron then to the large brown cabinet. Frustrated, I start from the opposite direction, the large brown cabinet, the dining room set, the settee. Wait. Is that a television?

Excitement builds in my chest. But we don't have any light. I have to ask Mama.

I turn, and Mama is standing behind me with a wide, silly grin.

"Mama. We have a TV? But we don't have any light," I squeal with confused excitement.

"Turn on the switch there." She points to the wall above the settee.

I flick the beige plastic switch, and a flood of light brings the room to life. I run to our bedroom. Flick. The spare room. Flick. Up. Down. Up. Down. I float back to the living room. Dada is now standing next to Mama, both tickled by my excitement. We all giggle before they lecture me about the added expense of having electricity and that it should only be turned on when it gets very dark.

For the first time, I look forward to nightfall. Each evening, I sit on the veranda and stare at the random blinking of firefly lights and wait impatiently for it to get dark enough for the lights to be turned on. I then hurry inside and settle into the warmly lit house for the rest of the night. No more flickering kerosene lamps. A few days later we get a refrigerator, which makes a loud humming noise. Mama fills it with milk, vegetables, eggs and meat.

However, the small black and white television set is the pride of our living room, and Mama and I can't get enough of the American shows that are broadcast from the two channels. Each night we surround its flickering lights, mesmerized and entertained. At first, I wrack my brain trying to figure out how the television works, but soon give up and get lost in the floating images moving on the screen—shooting, riding horses, running, singing and kissing in America. It all seems so magical. I can't wait to see America. I also see a new side of Mama. We are like two children, pointing and laughing at the antics of *Gunsmoke, Bonanza* and *The Andy Griffith* shows. On the weekends we watch together until they play the Jamaican national anthem before the station goes off the air at 11 p.m., leaving a grainy screen behind. Dada doesn't approve of televisions. It is not of Jehovah God, he would say. Mama would roll her eyes and kiss her teeth. She doesn't care what Dada or Jehovah approves of.

* * *

School is out for the summer. Mama, Dada and I are sitting at the back of the house one Saturday morning with both lazy dogs sprawled around us like furry lumps. She hums as she slices one side of a large orange-red mango and hands it to me. I bite into its sweet tangy flesh and the sticky juice crawls down my arm toward my elbow.

Dada chops long stalks of sugar cane. Lion and Jane Grip's ears stand at attention. They run toward the front gate, barking wildly. We hear voices. Mama and Dada hurry behind the dogs, who are going mad. I follow.

"Tap the noise!" Mama yells and shoos them before turning her attention to a tall woman with fair skin and curly black hair that settles at her shoulders. A young boy stands next to her, clutching an old-looking tan suitcase. Mama, Dada and the woman talk and laugh. I watch them curiously from the bottom veranda step as the boy peers from behind his mother and smiles at me. I smile back awkwardly.

Who are these people? They walk toward me.

"Donna, this is Lorna, your Uncle Clem's wife." I am more curious about the boy. Why does he have a suitcase?

Who is Uncle Clem?

"Mind your manners. What you suppose to say?"

"Hello, Miss Lorna." I pick at my fingers and glance at the boy, who is looking around.

"Hello, Donna. You get so big and nice." She stoops down and smiles at me. I smell her perfume. I feel Mama watching me.

"Thank you, Miss Lorna."

"This is your cousin, Sherlock," Mama says as she takes Sherlock's old tan suitcase from Miss Lorna. "He's going to live with us for a little while."

My belly bubbles excitedly at the thought of having someone to play with besides stupid Lion and Jane Grip. "Hello, Sherlock."

"Hello, Donna." He giggles.

The grown-ups walk into the house and Sherlock and I sit on the bottom step of the veranda. I study his round face. Full dark eyes and a thick top lip that curves downward.

"How old are you?" Sherlock asks, studying my face. The dogs gawk at him curiously from across the yard.

"I am eight. How old are you?" I smile shyly at him.

"I am seven, but me soon turn eight. Why oonu live near the cemetery?" Sherlock changes the subject and points to a row of tombstones.

"Don't you know is bad luck to point at the grave them?" I warn him.

"Me don't believe that foolishness. So why oonu live so close to the graveyard?"

"I don't know. Ask Mama. Why you come here to live anyway?" I put my hands on my hips and roll my eyes.

"Why you come here to live? Mama is my grandma, too." He shoots back with a grin.

"Me never ask you all of that. Me just ask you why you come here."

"And me answer you." Sherlock sucks his teeth.

"You fresh and out of order. I hope the dog dem bite you." We both look at Jane Grip and Lion, who have lost interest and are dozing in the shade. We giggle.

"What is yuh last name?" Sherlock asks as he tosses a rock at a tiny green lizard.

"Pinnock. What is yours?"

"Holmes." He grins.

"Sherlock Holmes? Like the detective man from foreign?"

"Yes, but the black one." We laugh and laugh and laugh until my head hurts.

I take Sherlock on a tour of the yard. We walk down the grass path leading toward the cow and pig pens. The cows look bored, and the pigs are asleep in the mud. Twinny, our donkey, glances in our general direction as we walk past the ackee and mango trees.

"Make sure yuh give Mama all the ripe mangoes so she can take them to the market to sell dem." I say as Sherlock looks up at the tree, searching for a ripe one. "If you eat them, she will lash you with the strap."

"She have to catch me first," he boasts. I ignore him and point out the outhouse.

"This is the latrine and down the road is the standing pipe where we get water."

"Donna and Sherlock!" Mama and Aunt Lorna are waving at us from the veranda. We race toward them. It is time for Aunt Lorna to leave and Sherlock follows her to the gate. She bends down and speaks to him softly. I can tell that he is crying.

She wipes his face and kisses his forehead before starting down the hill. I find myself wondering if my mother kissed my face and held me close, before she left me when I was a baby.

I study Sherlock from the veranda. He leans against the gate and gazes at his mother as she moves down the hill and onto the main road. When he could no longer see her, he sits on the ground by the gate and tosses pebbles in the bushes. I walk over to him.

"You alright, Sherlock?" I ask, studying his face, still wet with tears. "Mama wants you to come inside."

He wipes his face, stands and grins at me as if nothing happened. I smile back at my cousin and we race each other into the house.

We watch Mama as she empties Sherlock's suitcase and puts his clothes away neatly in the mothball-laden drawers in the extra room. School uniform, shoes, briefs, socks, pajamas, marina, and a school bag with pens, pencil, erasers and notebooks.

"You have to help Dada milk the cows and feed the pigs and goats dem in the mornings. When the mango drop off the tree, put them in the pan by the side of the house near the steps. You can eat all the bad ones, but if you eat the good ones, I will beat your likkle backside!" Mama points her finger in his face.

He glances at me and I stick my tongue out at him from behind her.

"The two a oonu will sleep in this room," Mama continues, "and oonu better make up the bed in the mornings." Sherlock smiles and makes a silly face when Mama bends down to close the drawer. She catches him. "Don't act like likkle hooligans, because me no fraid fe beat oonu likkle raas!" She stands and removes the wide leather belt from behind the door. I look over at Sherlock, who is no longer smiling.

"Yes, Mama."

"Yes, Mama."

After Sherlock comes to live with us, the empty loneliness to which I have become accustomed is gone. I don't think about my mother and father as often and I rarely pray to their pictures. I like having someone to talk to. I tell him about my mother, who lives in Kingston with my older sister, but I don't know much about my father. Sherlock has an older sister and a younger brother who live with him and his mother in Montego Bay. His father lives in foreign.

We carry water from the standing pipe, play police-and-thief and chase each other around the house. We wrestle on the veranda until beads of sweat glisten from our spent bodies or until Mama screeches "Oonu stop the blastid noise!" at us.

One afternoon Mama catches Sherlock eating a ripe mango that he knocked off the tree with a stone. Mama tries to chase him, but he is too fast. She throws a mango at him and it slams into his back as he turns the corner. He falls and a big coco lump forms on his forehead. He won't stop crying. Except for the day when his mother left, I have never seen Sherlock cry.

Although Mama gives him some sugar water to calm him down, he tucks in the corner of the red veranda, faces the wall and bawls. I move over and sit next to him.

"Leave me," he whines and tries to push me away.

"Sherlock, you alright? Stop cry nuh man."

"Me want to go back to my own mother," he sobs.

I know that Sherlock did not come to stay forever, but this is the first time that I am forced to think that he could leave. I don't want him to ever leave.

"Mama didn't mean it, Sherlock. You just have to listen better. Don't eat the good mangoes no more, okay?" I touch the lump on his head ever so gently.

"Me want me own mother." He pushes my hand away.

"Me want mine, too." I lean against him and this time he lets me. We both cry for our mothers.

"Wipe you face before Mama beat us with the belt." We pull apart and wipe our faces. We sit in silence and watch as a line of ants crawl out of a crack in the wall and disappear over the ledge.

Five

SILENT
GOODBYES

SHERLOCK AND I SETTLE INTO OUR RHYTHM. We walk to school and do our homework together on the veranda. We sleep and play together. We argue about everything—who is taller, runs faster, is better looking or a better singer. We sit under the shade of trees and make up fantastic stories about the lives we will one day have in foreign. The sun is trying to burn holes through our skin as we climb the hill after many trips to the standing pipe.

"Oonu stop and come here," Mama calls from the back of the house as we empty our buckets into the drum pan. We try to outrun each other to Mama, who is sitting on the back step. She looks up as we run toward her.

"Yes, Mama?" Sherlock and I answer in unison.

"Donna, your mother is coming next month with your sister and your new baby sister." With that Mama tucks an envelope in her pocket and enters the house. I stare at her back in a daze, a smile creeping across my face.

I knew Mommy was coming for me.

"Shut your mouth before a fly drop in it!" Sherlock's voice drags me back and I jump up and down with excitement.

I am finding it hard not to take flight from my skin during the weeks leading up to my mother's visit. All I can think of is being near her and my sisters. It has been six years since my mother came and took my sister. Mama says that she has been back to visit me, but I have no memory of her and just a vague recollection of my older sister. And now I have a new baby sister! I couldn't peel the smile from my face if I tried.

Two days before their arrival, there is a flurry of activity around the house. Mama cooks ackee and saltfish, roasted breadfruit, curry goat, stew chicken, peas and rice and cod-fish cakes. She bakes bammy and cassava pudding. Dada brings hard-dough bread, bulla cake, cheese and a jug of sorrel from the market. An assortment of coconut drops, gizzada and duckanoo line the wooden kitchen table. Sherlock and I help Mama to clean the floors, change the sheets, dust the furniture and sweep up the yard. Dada cuts the grass with his big machete and polishes the veranda until it glistens.

The night before my Mother and sisters' arrival, Sherlock and I lie in the dark, too excited to sleep. We can hear Mama and Dada's soft chatter coming from the living room.

"Do you think she is going to bring me a dolly, Sherlock?" I whisper in the dark.

"How me fi know?"

"What do you think she looks like?"

Sherlock climbs out of bed. There is just enough moon-light for me to see his wide grin.

"I think that she is going to act stoosh in her fancy Kingston clothes and high heels." He whispers and stands on his tippy toes, sticks out his chest and sashays across the floor with his butt in the air. I plant my face in the pillow trying hard not to laugh. "She is going to come on the veranda with her stoosh self and pointy pike heel shoes and fall flat pon her backside."

Sherlock flails, pretends to slip and throws himself across the bedroom floor. We burst out laughing.

"Tap the noise before me come in there with the belt!" Mama's voice rings in the night air.

Sherlock jumps back in the bed. We can't stop laughing. We fall asleep wishing that it was already tomorrow.

The next morning, we fly out of bed without any nudging from Mama or Dada. By mid- morning all of our chores are done.

"What time are they coming?" I ask Mama

"Dem soon come. Go bathe." She places the metal washtub behind the old kitchen and fills it with water from the drum pan. After my bath, Mama combs and brushes my hair, then makes two plaits that fall down on either side of my face. She secures them with two clear bubble clips at the ends. The water she mixed with Ultra Sheen and smoothed over my hair, gives it a shiny slick look. Mama pulls my red dress with little white flowers over my head, being careful not to mess up my hair.

After she zips up the back, I sit on the bed and fasten my white sandals. Sherlock is sitting in the living room; he looks up when I enter the room with a silly grin. He looks nice in his black church pants, a white shirt and his black school shoes and blue socks. Mama pulls two of the brown iron dining-room chairs onto the veranda and tells us to sit and don't move. She doesn't want us to mess up our good clothes. I gaze through the trees at the dirt path that leads from the main road up the hill. The excitement that stirs in my belly is so intense that my ears buzz.

I see three figures approaching in the distance. My heart is trying to escape my nine-year- old chest. Mama must have been looking through the window, because she rushes past us and down the veranda stairs, through the gate and down the hill. Everything is happening in slow motion like a hazy dream. I feel myself stand as Mama rushes to meet a short woman with straight black hair. She is wearing an off-green dress that hugs her slender frame.

My mother.

A baby balances on her hips as she struggles with two bags in the other hand. A young girl with fair skin and long brown hair is walking beside her with a large suitcase in one hand and a large brown bag in the other. Mama takes the baby and one of the bags from my mother. They are getting closer and my heart is racing. I have always imagined that I would run into my mother's arms when I see her, the way they do in television shows when someone comes home after a long trip. But I am frozen in the spot on the veranda, unsure of what to do.

The woman in the picture on the wall is walking toward me. She is a younger version of Mama with high cheekbones and bright eyes.

"Hello, Donna. How are you?"

"Hello, Ma'am." I am not sure if I should call her Mommy.

She looks at Sherlock. "Mama, this is Clem likkle boy?" she yells back at Mama, who is rocking my little sister.

"Yes. That is Sherlock," Mama answers.

"Hello, Ma'am." Sherlock stares at her shoes and looks back at me. She is wearing black spike heels. I stifle a giggle as I think of Sherlock mimicking her last night.

"You remember your sister Grace, right?" my Mother asks. My older sister smiles widely at me as she places the bags on the veranda. I study her brown skin and full eyes. Thick brown plaits extend down her back.

"Yes, Ma'am," I lie. I don't really remember her, yet I feel as if I know her. I smile back at my big sister.

"And this is your likkle sister, Lisa." My baby sister's chubby fingers are curled into the collar of Mama's dress as she screams and tries to squirm out of her arms, reaching for our mother. She looks like a big squirmy dolly. I stand still in the scene around me.

Grace and Sherlock are playing with lazy Lion and Jane Grip, who are being nosy, smelling everybody and everything. My mother walks past me, enters the living room and plops down on the couch. Mama follows her.

"Mama beg you for something to drink?" My mother reaches for my baby sister. Mama returns with a mug of water. My baby sister drinks from her bottle and plays with her toes and I watch my mother. I want to sit on her lap. I want her to ask me about school. I want us to hug. I want to ask her if I am going back to Kingston with her. But she is busy right now. Maybe later. I smile through the heavy disappointment that stirs within me.

After my baby sister settles down, my mother and Mama pry open the large brown barrel that arrived last week and has been sitting in the corner of the living room. It is full to the brim with bright shiny things. Sherlock, Grace and I watch from the doorway as they remove clothes, shoes, socks, pajamas, shirts and dresses. They make neat piles on the settee. My mother calls me over and hands me clothes with the tags still on them, a pair of pajamas, jacks and bubble clips for my hair.

"Have you been keeping up with your studies?" she asks.

"Yes, Ma'am." I want to wrap my arms around her. I don't.

"You been behaving for Mama?" She doesn't really smile. Her face is sunken into a strange grimness.

"Yes, Ma'am."

She nods approvingly and calls Sherlock over. And just like that, the conversation is over. My heart sinks deeper into my chest as I move away clutching my pile, wishing I could tell my mother that I have a gaping void that only she can fill. My mother stays with us for a week.

She spends most of her time with Mama, laughing, talking and cooking.

Sometimes I stare at her from a distance, watching her every move, drinking her in. Grateful for each interaction, which are few and sparse. I want to throw my arms around her and tell her how much I have missed her, but somehow, I know that she wouldn't be interested. Our plump cousin Cindy, who lives in town, stops by with her two daughters to visit our mother a few times.

Mama, my mother and Aunt Cindy sit on the veranda and drink sorrel and eat sugar cane. They laugh loudly and share stories about their youth in Duncans, Obeah and men. My sisters, Sherlock, our two cousins and I play in the backyard, because we are not supposed to listen to grown people's conversation, although we can hear everything they are saying. I just wish that my mother would laugh and talk with me like that.

It is the fifth day into her visit, and we are all walking home from Silver Sands Beach. Mama and my mother are walking ahead with my baby sister while Sherlock, Grace and I linger behind and play a guessing game where we try to predict the color of the next car that will drive by. My mother slows down and walks back to us.

"Oonu look out for the cars and pay attention." She gazes down at us.

"Yes, Ma'am." We answer in unison. She walks alongside us for a few yards before she speaks.

"Mama said that Grace and Lisa can live here with you all for a while."

"We're staying here?" Grace asks. I study her face and the smile that is trying to escape.

"Yes. I am going to New Hampshire in America to work for a while." We arrive at the bottom of the hill and hurry across the road. My mother continues. "Make sure you all behave yourselves for Mama. I don't want to hear no foolishness."

"Yes, Ma'am."

A wide smile is trying to crack my face as we climb the hill toward the house. My insides are squealing and shouting with delight as we enter the gate. My sisters are staying! My sisters are staying!

My mother returns to Kingston on the eighth day. No hugs. No kisses. Just more warnings about being good for Mama. A few weeks later, Mama tells us that our mother has arrived in New Hampshire to take care of white children.

* * *

I didn't think that I could ever be happier than the day Sherlock came to live with us. But I am. I love having my older sister Grace with me. She reads all the time. While Sherlock and I are running around like wild hooligans, her head is lost in a book. Love stories and mysteries are her favorite. We play games, hopscotch, nursery rhymes, climb trees and catch lizards. We wrestle on the veranda, play jacks by moonlight and watch American shows with Mama until sign-off. We fight sometimes, but for the most part we learn how to get along. I fall asleep each night, already looking forward to sunrise and the chance to play some more.

Grace and I take turns taking care of our baby sister, Lisa, whenever Mama is busy. At night we drink hot Milo and eat soda crackers in our pajamas before getting ready for bed. Grace is in the extra room with our baby sister and Sherlock and I on the small bed next to Mama and Dada's bed.

On one typical summer night, the air is thick and heavy with heat and the night songs of crickets. Grace and I are jumping on the bed. We leap in the air with reckless abandon, the mattress springs squeaking below us.

"Tap di damn noise in there," Mama yells from across the yard. We ignore her. "Shhhhh. Stop making so much noise. Don't jump so hard," Grace warns me with a whisper.

"Yuh making noise, too," I remind her as we continue jumping. We start slowly at first and then the excitement takes over. We are almost touching the ceiling.

"Me not going to tell you again. Tap the blastid noise!" Mama's voice sings in the night air. We crumble in a laughing heap on the bed. Sweating and gasping for air. I step off the bed and peek out the door.

"She is not coming. She is still outside," I tell Grace.

"Okay. Let's jump some more, but don't make so much noise." Grace stifles a giggle.

Before long we are jumping and giggling again.

"Close your eyes when you jump. It's more fun this way." I urge Grace as I levitate, feeling dizzy behind closed eyes.

No response. I keep jumping. Eyes shut. *Whack!*

The leather strap lands across my back. I fling my eyes open and Dada is standing beside the bed, arms in the air. Panic fills me. Disoriented and dizzy from jumping with closed eyes.

Whack!

A second one lands across my legs.

I wince. My eyes scan the room looking for Grace. She is nowhere in sight.

I jump off the bed and run past Dada, who gets in one last lash which crashes against my shoulder. I rush out of the room and onto the veranda. Grace and Sherlock are two crumpled laughing piles, positively howling. Barely able to breathe. My back and legs sting.

"Why yuh didn't tell me that he was coming? Me hate you!" I whine and rub the back of my legs.

"That's what you get for closing your eyes. Fool Fool, pickney!" Grace punts back and she and Sherlock collapse in a new round of laughter.

I try really hard to hold my anger, but cannot help myself. I join them on the floor, our rich laughter echoing through the night air.

Soon Grace enrolls at William Knibb High School in Falmouth, and Sherlock and I return to Duncans Primary School. In the afternoons, we all sprawl across the veranda. The scent of floor polish tickles our noses as we do our homework or play with our baby sister, Lisa. The smell of Mama's cooking wafts through the air. Soon Dada will be home and we will have supper as one big family. I love my new life!

* * *

It's a rainy Saturday afternoon in August of 1973, and the extra bedroom echoes with our laughter. All four of us are playing on the floor as the rain batters mercilessly against the tin roof. I peer out the window. The day is gray and gloomy. Mama's flowers droop under the weight of the heavy water droplets.

Loud voices are coming from the living room. We tiptoe and peer through the doorway curtain.

My mother is perched on the edge of the chair. Her hair hangs in wet clumps around her face and water drips from her body onto the living room floor. My baby sister squeals and runs into our mother's arms.

"I was expecting you next month," Mama says, handing her a rag.

"Yes. Me know, but everything work out. So, me come sooner." Our mother looks over and beckons to us. My sister and I walk toward her and Sherlock hangs behind uncertainly. She inspects us.

"Oonu behaving for Mama?" she asks, looking us up and down. After her cold indifference two years earlier, I don't expect much. I don't say much.

"Yes, Ma'am," we answer in unison.

She talks about the two children that she used to care for. She calls them ungrateful wretches. I watch her mouth moving. I bite my lip, wondering why she is here. She removes toys and clothes from her suitcase and hands each of us a neat pile. Sherlock gets army men, little cars and shirts. Grace and I get the same things: two blue-and-yellow short sets, socks, blue clogs and white dolls with vacant blue eyes. I love my new clothes and shoes, but I don't know how I feel about the white doll with the tough pink skin, golden shimmery hair and blue eyes that stare creepily at me.

"Thank you, Mommy." I feel awkward standing in front of her, shifting my weight from one leg to the other.

"Go an put you all stuff away." She waves dismissively.

We fold and place our new clothes in the drawers in the extra bedroom before heading to the veranda to play with our new toys. Mama and my mother walk into the kitchen. I can hear their voices as I pull the comb through my doll's blonde hair, with the face turned away from me.

It is a warm Friday, and we are spending another glorious afternoon at Silver Sands beach. Our mother sits in the shade on a large orange-and-white towel as we run along the soft golden sand, splashing in the water, the coolness lapping at our feet in a steady rhythm. I savor each moment as I wiggle my hands in the water and scoop up handfuls of sand that I toss at my sisters and cousin. We squeal with laughter. My eyes drift over to our mother. Her arms are folded, and her eyes watch us from behind sunglasses. She smiles and waves at us. My insides are happy. The smell of the salty sea invades my nostrils as waves gurgle and splash frantically around us.

We walk up the hill toward Mama's house as the sun is beginning to set on the horizon, and it feels good to walk alongside my mother. I hold my little sister's hand as Grace and Sherlock race ahead. My mother is leaving tomorrow to go back to America, but I want this moment to last forever.

That evening she combs my hair. I feel happy and wanted as I sit on the floor between her legs. She sighs heavily as she parts my hair in four equal sections and smears coconut oil against my scalp. I close my eyes and lean my back against my mother. She smells nice, like powder mixed with perfume.

"You have soft coolie hair like your father," she says, and gathers and brushes a section of my hair until it is smooth.

"Where is my father, Mommy?" I wait to be told to stay out of grown-people business.

"He went to foreign. You will see him one day." Her openness surprises me.

So, I keep talking.

"Mommy, are you going to take me back with you to foreign?" I close my eyes and hold my breath.

"You'll come one day. Now go and put on your pajamas and go to bed. Goodnight."

"Goodnight, Mommy." I fall asleep next to Sherlock, never having felt closer to my mother.

The next morning, we all get dressed and have breakfast in the dining room, which is usually only for special occasions. The air is thick with the aroma of ackee and saltfish, fried breadfruit and dumplings. My mother spreads a piece of butter on a slab of warm bread and hands it to each of us. My baby sister drinks from her bottle, which is filled with condensed milk and water, the only thing she will ingest without a fight. We eat hungrily before taking our empty plates to the kitchen and heading to our favorite spots on the veranda. My older sister buries her head in a Nancy Drew book near the top step, Sherlock sits on the ledge and I settle into the corner and comb the silvery blond hair of my doll. My baby sister tugs at Lion's fur, still drinking the sweet milk from her bottle.

We are still in the same positions when our mother steps on to the veranda fully dressed. Mama stands beside her.

"Grace, go and get your bags, they're on the bed." My older sister looks up from her book and stands looking confused. She walks into the living room and returns with her suitcase and another duffel bag.

My mother picks up my little sister and smooths her hair. I feel hot and dizzy.

"Come on," my mother commands, and Grace picks up the bag. I stand. I feel faint. I lean against the wall and watch in pained confusion. My mother kneels and buckles my little sister's sandals. I watch my mother's face, but she doesn't look at me as they walk down the red stairs.

The tears burn my eyes before bursting like water from a dam, spilling down my face.

"I am not going, too?" I ask no one in particular. I feel the muscles of my chin tremble as they walk toward the gate.

My mother says nothing to me. Mama walks behind them holding my little sister's hand as they make their way down to the main road. Sherlock and I watch from the veranda. I can barely breathe as I turn to Sherlock.

"Whe–where them going, Sherlock?" I stammer.

"Mama just told me that they are going to foreign," he mumbles. "Mama said that my mother is coming to get me today, too."

"How come is only me that nobody wants? Why everybody leave me?" I am crying loud and hard.

"Stop cry, man." Sherlock is behind me. His hand on my shoulder. "She will send for you. You wait and see. Soon you are going to live in foreign, too."

Later that day Sherlock's mother, Aunt Lorna, comes and Sherlock leaves with her. I watch his back as he walks down the hill. He turns and waves before they disappear behind the trees that hang over the lower part of the hill.

I settle into the corner of the veranda, my safe place when I am scared or lonely.

"Don't worry yourself. Your mother will send for you one day." Mama's voice fills the silence from the doorway.

"Yes, Ma'am." I stare straight ahead.

Mama goes back into the house, leaving me with the feeling as if I am a dirty, mangy, stray dog that no one wants. I stare at the red floor where we played jacks, wrestled, danced and laughed. I close my eyes and imagine that we are all together in America.

It's my birthday and we are celebrating in our mother's big fancy apartment in foreign. The music is loud and my skin tingles with excitement as we dance to a rhythm that fills us from head to toe. I can hear the hazy chatter of all the people who came to celebrate my birthday. My dad is dancing with my mother as they look lovingly at me. There is a large white cake in the middle of the table with my name spelled in pink icing and surrounded by all flavors of ice cream. Tomorrow we are going to the movies to continue my birthday celebration. Mommy, Daddy, Grace, Sherlock and Lisa form a circle around me. They are singing the happy birthday song at the top of their lungs. My face is bright and beaming.

I open my eyes and look around at the landscape of the countryside. The sun is beginning to set. The cows graze. The pigs wallow. Goats with long beards chew on leaves. The dogs smell the ground in search of food. The sun is beginning to set as a heavy and familiar silence crashes down around me. Life as usual in a day I will never forget.

Six

THE EYES OF
HANDSOME MEN

2016

I CHECK MY REFLECTION IN MY POWDER COMPACT. I am pleased with the golden-brown glitter eye shadow, cat-eye inspired liner, topped off with a delicate, pink-colored lip gloss. People hurry along the Upper West Side of Manhattan in the biting January cold as I wait for Javier De Leon from the Mount Hope section of the Bronx to arrive for our date.

We have been talking, texting and exchanging pictures for the past two weeks after meeting on Our Time, an internet dating website for folks over fifty. My stomach is in knots. I distract myself with the stunning array of colors that seem to jump off the walls of the Thai and Vietnamese restaurant. The waiter places two ice-filled, amber-colored glasses of water and menus in front of me. I draw lines along the condensation on one of the glasses and smile at a canoodling couple in a booth by the entrance. I nervously check my compact again and look down at my outfit: black slacks, black turtle-neck and my go-to olive-green leather jacket. Olive green is my favorite color.

I check my Fitbit. It is 6:21 p.m. He is six minutes late. My cell phone pings:

Wednesday, January 20, 2016
6:22 p.m.
Javier De Leon
Almost there. Few minutes.

I am processing a feeling of annoyance for his tardiness when the door chimes announce his arrival. His eyes scan the restaurant and I wave, recognizing him from his pictures. He waves back, smiles and walks toward me. I smile and do a quick scan. He is nicely dressed in a cream- colored sweater with a single black-and-brown button at the collar, blue jeans and a black leather jacket. He is shorter than I like, but he has a handsome face and there is something about his kind brown eyes.

"Nice to finally meet you, Donna. I am so sorry for being late," he apologizes and reaches out his hand.

"Nice to meet you as well, Javier." I shake his hand and he sits across from me. I take in his brown eyes and caramel skin.

Okay. This isn't so bad.

The waitress hurries over and places a complimentary bowl of fried onions between us.

"May I get you something to drink?" she asks, looking down at us with a wide grin.

Javier orders a ginger ale and I, my go-to drink, seltzer with cranberry juice. I push aside the fried onions and the glass of water to pore over the menu. I feel his gaze.

"You are very pretty."

I look up from my menu with an awkward smile. "Thank you. You're not so bad yourself!"

We giggle.

By the time his grilled pork chops over white rice and my sautéed eggplant with jasmine rice arrive, it is clear that we have quite a bit in common. He is also twice divorced, but with two sons, one about the same age as my daughter. He is only a year younger than me. We both love "Chandelier" by Sia, "All of Me" by John Legend, and "Loving You" by Minnie Ripperton. He has an adorable obsession with Anita Baker and attempts to sing "Sweet Love." A vocal disaster ensues, and we cackle.

I feel him studying me as I unwrap my knife and fork and lay the white paper napkin across my lap.

"On your Our Time profile, you wrote that you are a managing director for an international investment bank. What exactly do you do?" He unwraps his straw and dunks it in his glass of ginger ale.

"I am a senior human resources generalist."

He frowns with confusion.

"Hiring and firing. That sort of thing," I explain dismissively.

"Firing people must be tough," he says, wrinkling his face.

"It's no fun, but it goes with the territory," I reply, and take a delicate bite of the sautéed eggplant, even though I want to shovel it in. I am starving.

"So, what do you do?" I search his face.

"Well, I don't have a big fancy job like you," he grins. "But I am a private chauffeur and I have had Hoda Kotb, Tracy Morgan and Geraldo Rivera in my car. I was giddy when I met Hoda."

He chuckles and removes his phone from his pocket. He leans in across the table to show off the pictures of his celebrity passengers. He smells good. His hair is jet black and thinning in the front and his lashes are thick and long. I study his hands as he swipes from picture to picture. Clean and neatly trimmed nails. My eyes move back to his face.

I like him.

As we eat, he somehow manages to guide the conversation back to my job and the stock market. The topic sends him into a verbal and animated tizzy, as he rambles on about ETFs, CNBC, interest rates, IPOs, foreign exchanges and how skilled he is at picking winning stocks.

"I work in financial services and I don't share half your excitement about the markets," I observe. "So, tell me something." He looks up mid-bite. "Why aren't you working in the financial services industry if you have such a strong passion for the markets?"

"I guess I could if I really put in the effort," he replies. "I tried when I was younger, but I didn't want to make all the cold calls. That was stupid. It's too late now, because I am an old man, too old to start from the bottom." He dabs the corner of his mouth with his napkin and smiles crookedly. We finish our meal and he pays the bill with cash and asks if I would go with him to a lounge in the village. I feel fairly confident that he is not a serial killer, plus we are out in a public space.

"Well, since you asked nicely," I grin at him.

We get off the C train at West Fourth Street and walk along West Third until we are standing in front of the Fat Black Pussycat.

"What kind of place is this?" I ask, looking curiously at the large blue-and-white neon sign.

"Oh, Donna, it's just a lounge!" he chuckles as he takes my hand and leads me into the large, shadowy space with muted colors. Paintings and photographs line the walls and a large vintage chandelier hangs from the ceiling. Candlelight flickers on each table as couples nuzzle and whisper. Soft jazz plays in the background. I follow him down a small set of stairs to the lower level toward a back room hidden behind a dark red curtain. It opens up to a smaller space that boasts oriental rugs, lanterns and chairs with red velvet cushions that mimic royal thrones. We settle into a plush, orange-colored sofa and a waitress takes our order. We both order seltzer and cranberry juice with lime.

Neither of us drinks alcohol, which makes me think that we are going to get along very well. We talk. We laugh. He teaches me salsa, the bachata and dirty Spanish words. Four hours later we climb into the back seat of an Uber and head uptown. The driver pulls over at the corner of 86th and Lexington.

We hug, and he hops out and blows me a kiss. I settle into the soft leather of the SUV and watch him descend the subway stairs until he is out of sight. A smile creeps across my face as the Uber pulls away from the curb and I replay the date in my mind. His strong arms around my waist as we danced, the air thick with tenderness. The butterflies that fluttered around in my belly each time his soft brown eyes settled in mine. His voice. His face. I am beyond excited for our second date.

The doorman holds the door open for me with a smile. "Goodnight, Miss, Hayes. Have a good night."

"Thanks, Joe. You do the same." I check my Fitbit. It's 12:45 a.m.

Seven

SEVEN SUNSETS

1973

THE BRILLIANT RAYS OF THE JAMAICAN SUN caress our faces, as my best friend Naomi and I walk home from school on a Friday afternoon. We inspect the ground for rocks and toss them ahead, squealing and giggling as silly eleven-year-old girls do. We share a gizzada and say cuss words we are not supposed to say, like "bomboclat" and "raas."

"Guess what? My mother lives in New York at a place they call Brooklyn," I boast with a grin. "Soon she is going to send for me."

"So? My mother is going to send for me, too. But I am not going to no stupid Brooklyn, I am going to England, where everybody is stoosh and speaky-spokey." We crumble with laughter until we are too weak to walk without holding on to each other. We reach the intersection at Red Dirt, named for the bright, orange-colored dirt in the Parish.

My best friend Naomi moved to Duncans from St. Ann's about a year ago. She sauntered into my classroom with a silly smile, her shoulder-length jet-black hair held together with two large clear bubble clips. Loose hairs fell over her brown face as she moved between a row of chairs and plopped in the empty seat across from me. Scrawny legs dangled over the edge of the chair, barely touching the floor. She shot me a grin and I smiled back. We have been best friends ever since.

"Bye, Donna. See you in church on Sunday." Naomi wraps her arms around me; the scent of her hair pomade lingers between us.

"See you in Sunday school, crazy pickney." I force a smile as we pull apart and head in separate directions, the loneliness settling in. Now that my sisters and Sherlock are gone, I have come to depend on Naomi for company. I drag my hand along the tall blades of grass on the side of the road and watch them bend and glisten under the scorching sun. I stare ahead at the winding asphalt. Heat bounces off the surface, creating an illusion of quivering images. I cling to a memory of Sherlock and I walking home from school, laughing and running from Dr. Foote's big black ugly dog.

The sound echoes like thunderclap. I jump. A loud bang follows, and then the screeching of tires and crunching metal. A raw and primal scream rips through the warm afternoon and my eleven-year-old frame, like shards of glass. Ever so slowly, I turn my head toward the commotion and the blood drains from my face. Naomi's body is airborne. Her arms dangle beneath her and a lone yellow sandal twists and twirls in slow motion before settling on the hot asphalt. A scream tries but fails to find its way out of me as her head collides with the hood of a white mangled car. She twitches. My legs wobble. I want to go to her. I want to wipe the blood from her face, but my body is stuck in invisible quicksand. Everything feels slow and heavy. I am in a trancelike dream.

"Get up Naomi," I am screaming inside. "Please get up." My chest heaves and tears of shock flow in a heavy stream down my face but my arms are too heavy to reach up to wipe them.

My eyes cling to her twisted body and I find myself thinking of the first day we met.

There is a brief and chilling stillness. My pulse throbs loudly in my ears as feet stomp and voices shriek. Bodies push me aside. Someone yanks my arms and shakes me from the fog.

"Lickkle Pickney. You awright?" A short, plump woman with a red floral scarf wrapped around her head peers down at me.

"That is my—my fr—friend Naomi," I stammer and point toward the crowd gathering around her.

"Go home. Yuh shouldn't see this!" she scolds and tries to pull me away.

"No!" I protest, and dig my heels in, trying to pull away. I am not strong enough. I stumble and bounce against her bosom as the crowd grows. She smells like onions.

"Aren't you Miss Neomina's granpickney?" Headscarf woman asks demandingly. I glare in silent defiance. "Go home. Yuh don't need to see this. Go home. Right now!" Her voice is rich with authority.

I glance behind her in an attempt to see Naomi but a growing circle of frantic onlookers block my view. With one last desperate attempt, I try again to push past headscarf lady. She blocks my path and gently turns my head away from the direction of the commotion. I can't stop the tears.

Headscarf woman bends down and dabs at my face with a handkerchief. Her eyes have lost their harshness. She lowers her voice to an urgent whisper. I stare at the small wart on her nose. "Yuh fren gwine be awright. Deh gonna tek her to Falmouth Hospital. Go."

She takes my shoulders and points me in the direction of the road that leads to Mama's house. I realize that she is not going to give in, so I turn and shuffle slowly toward home until I can no longer hear the commotion or see the crowd that grows in the distance above the body of my best friend.

I sit on the veranda for hours and wait for Mama. Lion and Jane Grip are stretched out around me, sleeping. I try to process the mixture of sadness and shock that wrap around me, unable to shake the image of Naomi's crumpled body. I close my eyes and dream of the day when my mother will come back for me to live with her and my two sisters in Brooklyn. I try to imagine what New York City looks like as dusk falls heavily around me. The bright lights. The tall buildings. The rich people.

"Wake up Donna." My eyes pop open and my heart gallops. I can't see her face clearly, but Mama's sweet voice floats around me. Relief floods me as I leap to my feet in a fluster.

"Mama. Mama. Do you know what happened today? Naomi got hit by a car when we—."

"Me know," she interrupts. "She is unconscious in the hospital."

"Is she going to die?" I whisper and peer anxiously at her in the shadows.

"It is up to the good Lord. Come and eat yuh supper and go ah yuh bed."

She opens the door to the living room, and we walk to the kitchen together. I whisper grace above a bowl of rice and peas, chicken and callaloo and say an extra prayer for my best friend.

Naomi remains in a coma for three days, regains consciousness on a Monday afternoon and tells everyone that I pushed her in front of the car. My brain fogs with confusion when Mama tells me. Naomi would never tell a lie on me. Mama asks me again and again to explain what happened.

I tell her. Mama keeps me home from school.

One day a policeman strolls casually through the iron gate into our front yard. Jane Grip and Lion bark viciously.

"Good afternoon, young lady. Is your grandmother home?"

"She is inside, sir." I point toward the house as Mama emerges from the kitchen and shoos the dogs away with a red-and-white-checkered dishtowel.

"Hello, Mr. Constable," she greets him with an awkward-looking bow. He removes his hat and sunglasses before shaking Mama's hand. They whisper and look in my direction.

I look at my feet as my insides quiver. I have never been this close to a policeman. Is he here to take me to jail?

"Hello, Donna. I'm Constable James. Do you know why I am here?" Despite his very official presence, his eyes are kind. His voice, calm.

"Yes, Sir." I answer without making eye contact. I stare at a pile of ants gathering around something on the bottom step.

"Talk loud like yuh have some sense, pickney!" Mama grumbles.

"Yes, Sir." I speak louder, not taking my eyes off the trail of ants.

"It is such a nice day. Let's sit under that tree over there." He points his big shiny shoes in the direction of the large mango tree. I follow nervously. Mama hurries back inside, but I know she is peeping through the glass slats of the bedroom window. I sit down on one end of the large rock at the foot of the tree. He sits on the other and leans against its thick trunk. I pick at my nails and keep my eyes on the ground. My heartbeat pounds in my ears.

"Naomi said that you pushed her in front of that car. Tell me what happened."

"She is telling a lie, Sir. I did not push her. She is my friend." I keep my eyes on a small green lizard ambling by. My chin muscles tremble as I fight tears.

He removes a notebook from his pocket and writes frantically, punting questions at me about my school, friends, teachers and Naomi. Then back to more questions about the car accident that happened a week earlier at the intersection at Red Dirt. I answer the same questions over and over, just as I had in school the day Naomi woke up and told everyone that I pushed her in front of that car. The news had spread like wildfire through Duncans. I stood outside during recess and teachers and students circled me and pummeled me with questions.

"What happened to Naomi? She said that you pushed her," someone asked.

"You are lying! She didn't say that because I didn't push her. She ran across the street," I shot back. Confused.

"Then why would she say that you pushed her?" another voice shouted.

"I don't know. Why are you all telling lies on me?" I shout back.

"Why are you such a wicked little girl? Why did you do it?"

Question after question followed. I stopped responding. I pushed my way through the crowd and ran home as fast as I could, feeling scorned, helpless and confused.

I stare at the constable's mouth and I wish he would stop talking. I am tired and thirsty. I already told him all that I know. Over and over and over. Mama strolls by from time to time on the pretense of checking the dryness of the clothes that swing from the clothesline in the searing sun. After what feels like a very, very long time, he looks at his watch and stands abruptly. He tucks the notebook in his back pocket, returns his sunglasses to cover his kind eyes and faces me. I see my reflection in his sunglasses.

"Thank you, young lady." He smiles and angles his hat on his head. "Thank you, Ms. Neomina," he calls out to Mama as he moves toward the front gate. I watch him, unsure of what comes next. He stops and turns slowly to look at me.

"Do well in school, young lady," he says with a crooked grin. I nod and smile back at him sheepishly. The dogs eye him suspiciously with low growls as he moves through the gate. I return to sit at the tree's trunk and watch Mr. James' figure turn onto the main road in the distance. I told the truth. I hope he knows that.

The following Sunday, Mama doesn't take me to church with her. She says that she did not want to hear any more damn foolishness about me pushing Naomi. Church wouldn't be the same without Naomi anyway. We would sit side by side in our freshly pressed church dresses each Sunday and giggle and eat sweetie until someone shoots us an angry glare because the candy wrapper is making noise. Then we would stick out our tongues at the back of the person's head and giggle some more.

I chase the dogs around the house and read the Nancy Drew book that Grace left behind, to kill time until I see Mama walking up the hill. She looks so nice and dressed-up in her short-sleeved black dress and white hat with the black flower on the side. I walk down the hill to meet her. "Hi, Mama."

"That likkle pickney finally tell the truth!" Mama's face is twisted in anger. "Naomi told them that I didn't do it?" I feel as if I can't catch my breath.

"Yes. Oonu Sunday School teacher went to visit her in the hospital last night and tell her that if she lie, she will never go to heaven." Mama chuckles. "I guess she get scared of hell!"

"Mama! Why did she tell a lie on me in the first place? I thought she was my friend?" I want to scream.

"The likkle girl said that her blastid grandmother tell her to lie, to try to get money from your mother. I guess they know that she went to foreign."

My breath hitches as I recall the day I told Naomi that my mother moved to foreign. It was the day of the accident. We climb the rest of the hill in silence as I try to process the heaviness of betrayal that idles in my chest.

"Stay home and help me today." Mama is standing in the corner watching me as I get dressed for school.

"Yes, Ma'am." Quiet relief fills me. I just want to stay in the corner of the veranda away from everyone and everything.

"Don't take food or water from anyone," she continues. I know where this is going. "Don't let anyone comb your hair."

"Yes Ma'am." I feel the fear crawling over me as I study my grandmother's face. "Naomi's grandmother is talking 'bout putting Obeah pon you." Obeah is commonly used to settle differences. I have heard stories of people suddenly dropping dead, going bald or mad like our neighbor Miss Daisy, because of Obeah spells.

"She said that you will be dead in seven sunsets. But don't worry, I have something for her." Mama's face tightens in rage as she leaves the room. I fall asleep with terror twisting my insides.

A nudge to my back jerks me awake to see Mama peering down at me.

"Get up and put on your clothes." It is still dark outside. My lids are heavy. They close. Her voice drags me back to our bedroom.

"Wake up." She pokes me again. I sit up and try to rub the sleep away. She hands me my blue shorts and a white tee shirt. "There is a piece of hard dough bread and some hot Milo on the table." She walks into the other bedroom.

I eat in sleepy confusion as Mama ambles into the kitchen, dressed in her favorite brown dress with little pink and white flowers. Her face is lost under her tan wide-brimmed straw hat.

"When you're done, go to the chicken coop and get one of the chickens," she says nonchalantly as she peers at me from the rim of her tin teacup. I desperately want to ask why, but I am not supposed to question grown-ups, so I make my way over to the stinky chicken coop.

After much squawking and flapping of wings that leaves a swirl of dust, I am holding a nervous chicken against my chest as my grandmother walks out the front gate with us in tow. It is a chilly morning. We walk through the cemetery until we get to the main road. Mama hails a minivan. It is filled with hot and sweaty bleary-eyed people carrying boxes and bundles. The windows and seats rattle. We jostle from side to side as the van makes its way along the meandering country road. The stupid chicken won't stop flopping around and trying to escape. I search Mama's face, hoping that she will help, but she looks straight ahead and hums softly. I grab its legs firmly with one hand and shove my other hand under its wing, until it finally settles down.

Still not a word from Mama, just a blank stare. We disembark at a clearing and I watch the van disappear around a bend. The chicken is quieter now as it jerks and swivels its neck and head to look around. Mama walks a couple of feet ahead of me.

My dirty white canvas sneakers make imprints in the dewy soil along the gravelly terrain. Why are we here? More importantly, why are we here with a chicken?

A small hut with a roof thickly thatched with branches and leaves crouches in the distance. Mama is walking faster now. I linger behind her with sweaty hands that clasp the chicken, whose head is now hung low. The sun casts its golden rays across the top of the trees in the horizon as their branches sway rhythmically to the beat of a gentle breeze.

An image emerges in the distance. I squint. The person's footsteps are slow and halting. The figure gets closer. It's an old woman clasping a cane for support and shuffling toward us.

Her head is wrapped in a white turban and her long white dress has pearl buttons that travel up the front to meet a high-laced neckline, even in this heat. I linger behind as she speaks with Mama, who hands her an envelope, which she tucks in her brassiere. They speak in muted tones before the woman turns her gaze and hobbles toward me. I hold the chicken against my chest and close my eyes. I feel her hot breath as she removes it from my hands. I squeeze my eyes tightly.

"Open your eyes and look pon me." Her voice is coarse and gravelly. I don't.

"Open yuh eye, pickney!" Mama's voice sounds angry, so I open my eyes and allow tears of fear to escape. I look up at the woman in white. Her worn and expressionless face shines in the sunlight, accentuating the weathered lines in her skin. Her eyes, vacant.

"Take off all your clothes." She commands. Wait. What?

I search Mama's eyes pleadingly, and she nods approvingly. I am bawling uncontrollably as I remove my shorts, shirt and underwear. Mama takes them from me and kneels down to remove my sneakers. I hold on to her for balance, but mostly for comfort. I am confused and scared because I figured it out. This is an Obeah woman. The ones they tell children about in stories. The ones that can help you or hurt you.

Lady in White holds the flailing chicken in place on the ground with her bare foot, removes a knife from her pocket and with one smooth swoop, decapitates it. I jump. The headless bird bounces and flails, until its bloody white feathers are still.

Lady in White's eyes roll back, she frowns and whispers words I cannot understand before holding the chicken's carcass like a delicate teapot above my naked body and allows the hot blood to flow from the bird's neck and travel from my head down onto my chest and back and toward my feet. It is warm and sticky. Salty saliva thickens in my mouth. I stand still and stare straight ahead, at nothing in particular.

"This will protect you from Naomi's people." Mama's voice sounds distant as I pull up my shorts with sticky hands that won't stop trembling. I turn to watch the Lady In White shuffle to her hut with her cane in one bloody hand and the carcass of the headless chicken in the other.

We turn and walk through the bushes toward the road. Mama tells me that I cannot bathe for twenty-four hours or the spell will not work. My skin itches. We stand in silence under the hot sun as a van approaches.

I spend the next twenty-four hours in my favorite corner of the veranda, pushing the stupid dogs away, because they keep smelling me. I hate my mother for not taking me with her. If she had, none of this would have happened. I would be living in America, where they don't pour blood on scared little girls. The sun and the veranda are hot. Mama brings me cups of icy lemonade. My skin is caked with dry cracked blood, and the raw bloody smell makes me want to vomit out my insides.

Late in the afternoon of the next day, I sit naked in the zinc washbasin behind the kitchen. Mama hums as she lathers and scrubs my body from head to toe. Her hands move rapidly, and the warm sudsy water cascades down my body, softening the crusty layer that sits atop my skin. She tells me to step out and I look down at the reddish-brown water and my body feels weak as I remember yesterday. Mama pours a bucket of warm water over me, which feels great as it cascades through my hair down to my soapy little toes. She wraps a large or-ange towel that smells like carbolic soap around my shivering body, before slathering coconut oil all over me.

"You hungry?" Mama asks as she pulls my yellow sun-dress over my head.

"Yes, Ma'am."

"Go sit on the veranda. Me soon come."

I walk toward the front of the house feeling the breeze moving through my damp hair. A huge weight has been lifted from my shoulders now that the crusty smelly chicken blood and Naomi's people's curse have been scrubbed off of me. Seven sunsets came. Seven sunsets left. I did not die like the people in the stories that I have heard of. The Obeah Woman in White must have saved me from Naomi's wicked grandmother, and I am glad Mama took me to her. I look back at Mama, who is humming as she washes the basin, before turning it upside down and spreading the washcloth on top of it to dry in the afternoon sun. Mama meets me on the veranda and hands me a piece of coco bread with cheese. She begins to comb my hair. My legs dangle from the chair as I chomp happily. She hums "Jesus Keeps Me Near the Cross" as she bends over and places the large tooth of the comb at the tip of my nose and drags it down the middle of my head to make a straight part.

"In your life, always trust the good Lord. You hear me?" She rubs my scalp with coconut oil.

"Yes, Mama."

"The good Lord has been looking out for you from the day you came into this world. You got knocked down in the schoolyard," she pulls a bubble clip around the bottom section of my hair, "and almost bleed to death. Now this foolishness and the Lord saved you again. Get your book learning and trust God and nothing can harm you. Yuh understand?"

"Yes, Mama," I reply, settling my back into her softness.

A few weeks later, Naomi goes to live with her mother.

Eight

FLIGHT

IT IS APRIL OF 1974. I join the crowd of girls who form a circle around the *Jamaican Gleaner,* searching for our names among the long list of finely printed names of those who have passed the Common Entrance exam. Passing it would mean that I have earned a full scholarship to go to one of Jamaica's most prestigious high schools, and benefit from education not available in rural Duncans. It feels as if there are bricks in my stomach as I scan the pages. I use my index finger to follow each line of names that begin with the letter P.

Turn page. Scan.

Turn Page. Scan.

Turn page.

My heart races. Passing the common entrance is considered the ultimate milestone for Jamaican students. The thought of not finding my name terrifies me. Mama would be disappointed. I can almost hear her voice.

"Once you get your book learning, no one can take it from you."

After about three pages, I find it and breathe a sigh of relief. *Donna Pinnock.* I have been accepted to Westwood High School and will be a member of the incoming class of 1974.

I run through the gate and head straight for Mama, who is at the back of the house feeding the lazy dogs.

"Mama! Mama! I passed. I passed. I am going to Westwood." My throat is parched and the energy shooting through my body is electric. Mama stands and raises her hands toward the clear blue sky.

"Thank you, Sweet Jesus!" Her face splits with a wide smile. Then she turns to me. "That is a wonderful, wonderful thing, man. Thank the good Lord. When you going?" she asks, still beaming.

"I go in September, Mama."

"I am going down to Miss Ginny so she can write your mother and tell her." She hurries into the kitchen and in a few minutes, she is hurrying down the hill with a white pad in her hand. I enter the house to change out of my school uniform, grinning from ear to ear.

Several weeks later, on a Sunday morning, Mama gives me the best news as I am getting dressed for church.

"Your mother sending for you to spend the summertime with her in New York. You are leaving in July, before you start Westwood." She beams.

I feel as if the wind is knocked out of me. I sit on the side of the bed. "Really Mama? I am going to America?" I study Mama's smiling face.

"Yuh deaf? Yes, you going for the summer." She laughs. "Now hurry and go eat. I don't want to be late for service." She walks out of the room humming "Amazing Grace."

The sun creates a kaleidoscope of colors against the church's stained-glass window as we clap and sing "Pass Me Not, Oh Gentle Savior" along with the choir, who look like happy angels in their white robes. My insides dance with joy each time I think about going to America for the summer. I can't wait to see my sisters and walk along the bright, pretty streets of New York City. I can almost hear the cars honking and imagine that the streets are so packed with people that we have to weave between them like in the television shows. Maybe I'll go to a movie or a party. I can't wait to take a bath inside instead of behind the shed in the large metal basin. No outhouse in Brooklyn!

I am so excited that I feel as if I am about to leave my skin. So, I try to focus on the sound of the pastor's voice. He is talking about Jesus' love and how we must love our neighbors as we love ourselves. I am usually bored and fidgety by now, but today I hang on his every word, read along in the Bible and raise my hands in agreement as he shouts from the pulpit. I want God to know that I am thankful.

"God has not forgotten his people. Praise the Lord, church!" His voice fills the small room.

"Praise the Lord." My hands are waving in the air. "Hallelujah!" "Hallelujah!"

Shortly before my twelfth birthday, a barrel arrives from America on a Saturday afternoon. I giggle with excitement as Mama and I unpack the pretty clothes, underwear, shoes, training brassieres, sandals, a new suitcase and hair clips that my mother sent. I can barely contain my excitement about getting dressed up and going someplace nice in New York with my mother and sisters. To Mama's amusement, I pack the suitcase that very night, place it under the bed and wait for the day to arrive. I want my last day at Duncans Primary School to hurry and get here. I will miss my friends, but I can't wait to get to foreign. I count down the days with colorful markings in my school notebook.

* * *

It's finally here, a bright Saturday afternoon in July 1974. Everything looks shinier and brighter as Mama and I walk past the cemetery toward the bottom of the hill. My cousin Junior is leaning against his car smoking his pipe and takes one last puff as we approach.

"Hello, Mr. Junior," I say cheerily.

"Hello, young lady. Ready to go on the plane?" He grins at me.

"Yes, Mr. Junior," I reply as I climb into the back of his big blue car.

Excitement churns in my stomach as we drive through the countryside, past people going about their day, bundles on their heads, herding animals or selling sugar cane on the side of the road.

I want to scream out the window and tell everyone and everything that I am finally going to America.

A rush of exhilaration flows through me as I enter an airport for the first time. I am greeted by a cacophony of sounds as people spill from every corner of the space. I watch in wonder as a sea of faces mill about in organized chaos. They stand in lines, drag suitcases down narrow aisles that are decorated with faded posters. A faint aroma of food lingers beneath the bright overhead lights that bounce off gleaming white floors. Mama and I join a winding line and move our way up to the counter.

Soon Mama is telling me to go with God and handing my passport to a smiling stewardess, who leads me down a long corridor toward an open waiting area. I have never seen an airplane before, except for on television, and couldn't have imagined that they are this huge. They look like giant shiny metal birds outside the large waiting area window as they take off and land. My stomach churns with a mixture of excitement and terror. I push the fear down and try to think only of going to America to be with my mother and my sisters. A dream I have dreamt for as long as I can remember.

The stewardess directs me to a window seat in the middle of the Pan Am aircraft. I fidget as she secures my seatbelt, my heartbeat pounding against my chest. Large shiny metal birds are outside my window ready to fly to far-away places. A plump woman with her head neatly wrapped in a colorful scarf sits next to me with a warm smile. I jump at the sound of the door being slammed shut and she pats my hand reassuringly.

"You alright, man. No worry." She laughs, which causes her large breasts to bounce up and down. I smile back at her.

The engine roars to life and I dig my fingers into the armrests. Soon we are speeding. The force pushes me back against the seat. The plane rattles and lifts us above the ground and Jamaica pulls away beneath us. The view of houses and water and trees reminds me of a colorful postcard. America, here I come!

It feels as if we have been up here for hours, surrounded by clouds that resemble giant cotton balls. The engine hums, my ears pop and ache. I squeeze my eyes and try not to think about being in the sky, so I fantasize: *My sisters and mother are waving at me as I get off the plane. They hug me before driving me to one of those nice restaurants like the ones on TV to welcome me to America. Waiters in white shirts bring us fancy food on fancy plates. We eat and laugh, like one big happy family.*

I cannot wait to get off this plane.

A jolt. My eyes fling open. Then the sound of a loud bang echoes through the aircraft. Then a second bang and the plane wobbles with a strong vibration. The captain's voice sounds gravelly through the loudspeaker.

"There is a crack in the wing of the aircraft ... emergency landing ... Miami ... seatbelts fastened ..." His voice breaks up.

I hear a third thud and watch in confused horror as the stewardesses run along the aisle toward the front of the aircraft looking panicked. Passengers look around at each other nervously. The aircraft jerks violently and hurtles from the soft cottony clouds toward the water. The woman next to me pulls my seatbelt tighter and wraps her large arms around me. Our heads touch as she prays. We sob. The oxygen masks dangle in front of us and the lights go out. We are all screaming. Some beg God for mercy as luggage dislodges and becomes projectiles.

This goes on for what seems like forever, before it stops as suddenly as it began. We look around anxiously trying to peer through the pitch-black darkness of the aircraft. Are we dead in the water?

A slow burn of anger is building inside of me. How is this fair? After all this time of waiting, dreaming and hoping to see America, I may not get there? It may all end here in the cold metal darkness of the aircraft during my first time on a plane. A buzzing sound fills my ears as tears flow against the woman who holds me close to her. Maybe I only get two saves. God already saved me from dying in the schoolyard and from Obeah—maybe I don't deserve a third one. Still, I plead with Him to get me to New York so that I can see the lights, take a shower, hug my sisters and watch color TV. After all, I am only twelve and Mama said that I was special to God because he is going to use my life for his glory. So, this can't be it. It just can't. I cry hopeful tears in the dark eerie silence.

The lights flicker on and off and on again. There is a collective gasp as our eyes adjust to the sight of luggage and debris that litter the aisle. My throat feels raw from screaming and my head throbs as the captain's voice cracks through the loudspeaker. I feel disoriented.

"Stay in your seats with your seatbelts fastened." I peer out the window and sob with relief at the sight of lights in the distance. The plane rocks and shakes. I just want to get off.

I am not sure how much time passes before there is another jolt and then a loud thud as the wheels of the plane slam against the tarmac of Miami International Airport. We erupt in wild applause as the plane taxis to the gate. My mind jolts back to the day of the accident in the schoolyard when I was five years old. *The tall boy reaching above me trying to catch a ball and knocked me over instead. The feel of the pointed rock penetrating the lower left side of my head, the blood pooling around my neck and soaking my canary-colored uniform shirt. I can still see Dr. Foote's troubled look as he shone his bright penlight into my eyes. The room spins and I lose consciousness several times.*

Mama's sweet voice rings in my ear. "Remember that God save you for a reason. No matter what happen to you in life, never forget this day. You are a special child. If me don't know nutting else, that me know!"

I did not bleed to death in the schoolyard or die from an Obeah spell, and the plane somehow stopped free-falling. I am trying to trust God like Mama told me to, but I am filled with indescribable terror as we deplane and board another plane in Miami to take us to JFK, our original destination. I am sure that this time we are walking to our fiery deaths.

Relief surges through me like wildfire when we land in the darkness of John F. Kennedy International Airport. Ten hours late. I am practically running to keep up with the stewardess who is walking way too fast.

Gone is the wide smile that she welcomed me with when Mama handed me off to her in Jamaica this morning. She is now disheveled and somber as we hurry down a long corridor. She hasn't said much to me since we left the aircraft, and

I can't help but wonder if she is thinking about how close we came to death today. I know I am. My new patent leather shoes are torturing my feet and my head is throbbing. The bag with the jar of honey and snacks that Mama packed feels incredibly heavy. I struggle with it, moving it from one side to the other as I try to catch up with my stewardess with the stoic expression. The air is hot, heavy and smells like diesel fuel. We enter a large space in the terminal, and I am amazed at how many people there are. It is like a colorful sea of faces moving about in organized chaos. Old and young drag luggage behind them, some lounge on chairs and others appear to wander aimlessly. I already love America, even the airport. We walk past fancy shops, restaurants and food stands. There is unfamiliar music playing in the background, periodically punctuated by the sound of the planes taking off and landing on the runway tarmac just outside.

I can't ignore the nervous energy that flutters about in my belly each time I think about reuniting with my mother and sisters. It has been a year since they left on a sunny afternoon. Without saying goodbye. Without explaining why I had to stay behind. I push the painful memory to the side and thank God for stopping the plane from crashing so that I can finally see America.

We turn the corner and my mouth drops open. There is a very high and magical moving staircase on either side of me, one is going up and the other is coming down. People are stepping on and off nonchalantly, but I am terrified by the prospect. I look up to the face of the stewardess, and it is clear that she is not in the mood to entertain my hesitation. I step on awkwardly on the downward bound one—and for a few seconds, I don't know what to do with my hands.

The stewardess and I stand at baggage claim in uncomfortable silence for what feels like forever before the carousel finally spits out my luggage. Before long, I am hurrying behind her again as we walk toward a gated waiting area, my feet hammering against my shoes. I pick them out of the thick crowd. My mother and sisters are waving at me and I am suddenly nervous.

What if my mother is as distant as she was when she visited in Jamaica? What if she still doesn't like me? I really want her to like me, and maybe one day she'll let me live here with her and my two sisters. I wave back with a wide smile as we approach. The stewardess speaks quietly with my mother, hands her my passport and hurries away. My mother looks me up and down in horror and my sister giggles.

Honey is dripping from the bag, the front of my dress is stained and my afro is completely flat on one side from burying my head in the arm of the plump woman who held me close as our plane fell from the sky. They hang on my every word as I explain that the first plane was broken and almost killed everyone, and then I fell on my backside on the moving staircase causing the bottle of honey to break. I marvel at the fact that the bottle of honey survived the turbulence of an almost plane crash only to shatter on a magical moving staircase.

"It is called an escalator!" Grace rolls her eyes and giggles.

My mother throws her head back and laughs as well. My mother is laughing with us. Soon we are all laughing. I feel my entire body relax as we follow our mother out into the warm night air toward JFK's parking lot.

* * *

Life in Brooklyn, New York, is so different from Duncans. A jumble of buildings that resemble boxes of presents are everywhere. Telephones, hot showers and color television that never goes off. I wish I could stay here, where car horns blare and music coaxes children out to ice-cream trucks. Where streetlights come to life on their own when it gets dark. The next six weeks are like my own personal heaven. My mother is very different from the woman who stood on Mama's red veranda a year ago and looked at me as if I was some sort of strange specimen. She has gained weight and is kinder and sweeter. She takes me shopping for new clothes; she cooks almost like Mama and feeds us ice cream in black-bottomed glass bowls before bed. Sometimes we crawl into her bed and polish her nails while we watch television. For the first time, in my entire life, I feel as if I belong and I don't want this feeling to ever end.

One night, my older sister, my baby sister and I are sitting around the dining room table, showered and dressed in our pajamas and devouring bowls of vanilla ice cream. My mother leans against the refrigerator. I feel her eyes on me.

"So, I hear that you are going to Westwood," she says with a smile, studying me.

"Yes, Ma'am." I slurp another spoonful of the sweet creamy mixture.

"It is a very good school. Make sure you do well with your studies."

"Yes, Ma'am." I wish I had the courage to say what I really feel. That I want more than anything to live with her. But I don't.

When Mommy goes to work, we eat sugary cereal, experiment with each other's hair, sing disco songs, dance the bump and the hustle and watch endless hours of TV. My favorite show is *The Price Is Right*. I love to watch the contestants bolt out of their seats and charge down the aisles to bid on televisions and cars and pretty watches. I daydream of owning the pretty things that cover the stage of my favorite game show.

Three weeks after my arrival, my mother makes a stunning announcement on a Friday evening. Grace and I are sprawled out on the living room floor watching television. Our baby sister naps on the loveseat. "Your father is coming to see you and Grace tomorrow." Her tone is so matter of fact, that I am sure I misunderstood.

"Did you say that our father is coming? Here?" I sit up and study her with excitement brewing in my stomach.

"Well, that's what he said. He wants you two to meet him in the lobby at three o'clock tomorrow afternoon," she responds nonchalantly.

"I am finally going to meet him?" I am finding it hard to grasp what she is saying.

"Meet him? Well he was there when you were born." She chuckles. "And he came to see you one time at Mama's house.

"He did?' When?" I asked, looking from my mother to my sister.

"I remember," Grace chimes in. "Donna, you were too young, so that's why you don't remember."

"I do remember a man standing on the veranda when I was a little girl. He had a very big afro and he gave me an apple."

"Yup. That was him!" Grace shrieks.

"That was our father? Well, how come he never came back to see us?"

"You will have to ask him that." Mommy snickers.

For most of the night, I lie awake excited about seeing my father and trying to process the fact that he came to visit me in Duncans, but I had no memory of him, until today. Secretly fuming and disappointed. He knew where I was all this time, but for some reason, I was not worthy of his time. That familiar stray-dog feeling hovers.

That afternoon, I step out of the elevator into the lobby with my heart in my mouth. The idea that I am getting ready to see my father is overwhelming. My sister and I walk side-by-side toward the entrance.

"That's him. Standing next to the black car. That's Daddy." Grace nudges me and points at a tall man with curly hair. Our father is in his early thirties and even more strikingly handsome than the picture of him that hangs on the bedroom wall at Mama's house. I gawk at him. He is probably the most handsome man I have ever seen. He has dark brown eyes and thick brows. He is light skinned like Grace, but his hair is curly and wavy like mine.

"Hello, Grace and Donna." My father smiles at us with perfect teeth.

"Hi, Daddy," we respond.

"You girls are getting so big. Kiss mi foot." My sister and I giggle at his use of an expression that is used to convey shocked amusement. An expression that I will come to associate with my father. I study him as he throws his head back and laughs. There are so many things that I want to say and scream at him, but I don't dare. Children's feelings are to remain inside.

"So, Donna, how do you like New York?" He gazes down at me.

"I like it very much and want to stay forever," I respond emphatically.

"You have to go back to finish school," Grace chimes in annoyingly.

"I heard that you got into Westwood. That is a very good school," Daddy says before walking over to the driver's side.

"Yes, Sir. I did." Surprised that he knows anything at all about me.

"Okay. Let's go."

Grace climbs into the front and I settle into the soft leather in the back seat. Our handsome father pulls out into traffic. I study the curly hair at the nape of his neck, his strong profile, and the sparkly ring on his pinky finger—before shifting my gaze to the changing scenery of the Brooklyn streets, feeling as if I am in one of my fantasies. Daddy fiddles with the radio until reggae music fills the car. We bob our heads and sing along with Bob Marley.

My father asks about my mother's new boyfriend and father to our little sister. We don't say much. Mommy warned us not to tell him her business. He mentions that we have several other siblings and I wonder if he ever sees them.

We pull into the drive-thru of a place called Burger King. Daddy orders cheeseburgers, french fries and thick shakes. I have never had fast food before, just Mama's glorious cooking. Yet, there in the back of my father's car, the aroma fills the air and I find myself salivating in anticipation of this strange New York food. I take a bite and can't believe how delicious it is.

The juicy burger with gooey melted cheese and pickles sandwiched between a warm soft bun with some sort of seeds on it. A tangy sauce drips through my fingers as I chomp on long pieces of deep-fried potatoes, drenched in ketchup. I sip on my vanilla shake and gaze out the window, wishing this fantasy day with my father and sister would never end.

My father drives us to Coney Island. It is my first time at an amusement park, and I am once again wide-eyed with giddy excitement. My smile grows wider as I struggle to process it all. The bright, colorful and flashing lights, happy squeals of excitement, music emanating from various sources, and the night air, thick with the smells of different foods. I feel as if I am transported to a colorful fantasy world that has taken my breath away. Soon my sister and I are getting dizzy on spinning rides. We hold on to each other, our cheeks flushed with excitement as our roller coaster crawls up steep tracks before tossing us precipitously toward the ground, our shrieks pierce the night air. We chomp on cotton candy and play games in hopes of winning one of the large stuffed animals that seem to smile at us from the top shelves.

Our father pulls up in front of our mother's building around 8 p.m. My sister and I hug him before we enter the marble-floored lobby, struggling with the giant green teddy bear that my sister won at the amusement arcade. Although we are grinning from ear to ear, a pang of sadness is crawling around in me, because I know that my summer vacation will come to an end in a couple of weeks. And the last thing I want to do is to return to Jamaica.

I want to stay here in Flatbush, Brooklyn, continue to get to know my family and live this perfect summertime daydream.

"Where are my nieces?" Our uncle's booming voice fills the apartment on a Friday evening.

"Uncle Errol! Uncle Errol!" we squeal with delight as we rush excitedly down the hallway into his wide hug.

My mother's younger brother lives right next door with his wife. We love when he visits! He lives for pranks, lame jokes and exaggerated dance moves that make us all collapse with laughter. He makes summer vacation Friday nights extra fun.

"Hey, big girl!" He picks up our baby sister, Lisa, and gives her a peppermint candy. She promptly unwraps it, pops it into her mouth and hands him the wrapper. Uncle Errol tips his head back and fills the apartment with laughter. I look forward to this Friday night ritual of our uncle playing reggae music on the turntable as my mother, sisters and I sing at the top of our lungs, and twirl and twist to the rhythm in the middle of the living room floor.

Although my uncle owns his own barber shop, writing and arranging music is his passion. He plays "Gun Fever" repeatedly, a famous song that he penned. He alleges that he knows Bob Marley, taught him how to sing and helped him with his musical arrangements before he became famous. We all secretly believe that he is exaggerating, until the afternoon my uncle's doorbell rings and Bob Marley and two men are standing on the other side, wide smiles flashing from beneath thick black dreadlocks. My breath quickens.

Grace and I can't believe that we are looking into the handsome face of the man who sings some of our favorite dance music. Yet, for some reason, my sister looks as uneasy as I feel around them. Maybe it's their "bad boy" swagger, the lawless energy or the wild hair that resembles small, thick tree branches. They shake hands with a gushing Uncle Errol before sauntering past Grace and I, shoulders back with long strutting steps toward the living room. My eyes follow them as they settle on the plastic- covered settee. Uncle Errol leans back in his chair and laughs and talks excitedly with his famous friends. They don't notice when we sneak out quietly and close the door behind us to return next door to our mother's apartment. He does know Bob Marley!

I can't wait to tell Mama and the girls at Westwood.

I want to be as nonchalant on the inside as I appear to be on the outside as I pack my suitcase, but I don't want tomorrow to ever come. I smile through the sadness of a twelve-year girl who is secretly begging God for a miracle—a miracle that would make her mother tell her that she can stay. I know that asking to stay in New York after being awarded a scholarship to Westwood would be considered ungrateful, so I wear my mask of calmness and indifference, a heavy sadness burning my chest.

The next morning, I climb into the backseat of my baby sister's father's car. The ride along the summer streets that lead to JFK airport is almost unbearable. We step out into the August heat. The sweet memories of the summer well up in my eyes as we walk toward the ticketing counter in silence, my baby sister holding my hand. I hug them with a forced smile and head toward my departure gate.

Nine

THE RIGHT TO
REMAIN SILENT

IT HAS BEEN A MONTH SINCE MY FIRST DATE with Javier De Leon, and there have been many more since. We go to movie theaters, engrossed in the pictures on the screen and each other's presence, eat in restaurants with salads and pasta dishes between us and take long walks along the East River. Javier is mild-mannered, intelligent, chivalrous, and downright sweet.

I am praying for good news as I pace back and forth in my office. I stare at my computer screen, unable to focus, foot tapping up and down as I wait for my daughter Ava's call. I can feel the fear in my chest trying to take over. I let out a slow controlled breath and try to focus on the memo on my screen. I jump at the shrill ring of the phone. I glance at the console. It is 10:15 a.m.

"Hey baby." I close my eyes and take deep slow breaths.

"Hi Mom." Her voice sounds heavy.

"What did you find out?" I ask, trying not to leap out of my skin. My daughter works for an investigative services company.

"I am so sorry, Mom, but the man you met on Our Time is a convicted felon." A cold sweat covers my skin. "He served six years in a federal prison for a 1992 armed robbery of a bank in Lake Worth, Florida."

I hear the regret in her voice. She knows my plight more than any other living person. "Are you sure it's him, baby?" I croak.

"Yes, I'm sure, Mom. I ran the report five times. It's definitely him."

Tears well up and I fight them.

"Mom, are you still there?" I can hear the concern in her voice.

"Yes, baby. Thanks for doing this. Let's talk later, okay? Love you, baby girl."

"Sure, Mom. I am so sorry. I love you, too."

The line goes dead.

I stare at the phone for a while, trying to process my conversation with my daughter. I type Bank Robber. Lake Worth. Florida 1992, into the search and hit enter. The following article appears in front of me:

> Police in Puerto Rico and the FBI have arrested a man they believe helped rob a Barnett Bank branch in Lake Worth, Florida in January.
>
> According to the Palm Beach Sheriff's Office, Marco Escano, 30, and Javier De Leon, 28, both of Springfield, wore ski masks and brandished semiautomatic pistols when they robbed the bank. The FBI said the men forced six employees and 22 customers to lie down on the floor at gunpoint.
>
> While Escano guarded the door, De Leon leapt over a teller's station and ordered two tellers to turn over the money from their cash drawers. No one was hurt.
>
> Escano, 31, was arrested on Saturday morning while asleep in a house in Puerto Rico, FBI spokesman Albert Olson

said. DeLeon was taken into custody in New York in February when he was stopped for driving a stolen car. De Leon rented the car after the robbery but never returned it. The police recovered nearly $10,000 in cash from the robbery at the time of his arrest.

Both men were identified as suspects after a witness recognized them with their masks off as they were changing cars at an apartment complex about two miles from the bank, police said.

Ava had recently graduated from Point Park University with an undergraduate degree in English and landed a job in the call center of a background investigative firm. I thought it would be fun for us to play private investigator and run free background checks on ourselves, my ex-husbands, my high school bullies and on Javier—my boyfriend of one month. The idea of secretly prying into his background felt creepy, even though the information is public.

What was intended to be harmless and playful fun has produced shocking and devastating results. My belly feels like a ball of tangled yarn. Everything has been going exceptionally well with Javier. I hurl questions at myself. Was this a huge mistake?

Should I wait for him to come clean? What if it wasn't him? My hands shake as I dial Javier's number.

"Hey, my beautiful *chica*. Do you miss me?" he asks flirtatiously.

I answer a question with a question. "Are you an ex-con?" I spit the words.

"What are you talking about?"

"I did not stutter, Javier. Are you an ex-con? More specifically, did you ever rob a bank?"

"What are you talking about?" he repeats.

"That's a yes or a no!"

"I have never robbed a bank," he snaps.

"That's the story you're sticking to. Correct?"

"Look, *chica.* Javier De Leon is a very common name. There are so many people sleeping in cold cells right now because of mistaken identity. It was not me!"

I can hear the anger in his voice. I want to believe him, but it is all too coincidental.

"Well, someone with your name, address and date of birth robbed a bank twenty-two years ago. How do you explain that?" I close my eyes and resume the deep breathing.

"Did you do a background check on me?" He sounds offended. I remain silent.

"Can I come to your job and take you to lunch today? We need to talk." There is a sudden urgency in his voice.

"Nope. I have a business luncheon today. We'll talk some other time."

"How about tomorrow night? I can come by and cook dinner for you."

I am smitten with Javier, and I want to give him the benefit of a doubt because he just doesn't seem like the type of person who would do such an awful thing. And I think I have fallen in love with him. I want to hear what he has to say. Or do I? My conflicting emotions are like charging horses pulling in opposite directions. After having my heart stomped on by other loves, I need to do everything within my power to protect myself. I want to dismiss him with abject nonchalance—after all, I am a Wall Street executive, a one-woman-show performer and a marathon runner. I am no longer the fragile, broken woman who shows up in a diminished way, needy and desperate for attention. Yet, I hear my voice as if it were not my own.

"Fine. See you tomorrow." I hang up.

The following evening, I stand where we agreed to meet

at 6:15, in front of Whole Foods at the corner of 88th Street and Third Avenue to buy the ingredients for his dinner. I pull my scarf snugly around my neck and check my watch. He is eight minutes late. Annoyance is creeping around my belly. People on cellphones, with puppies, children and packages, hustle by. There is a sick feeling in my stomach. Tugging at me. My phone pings:

Wednesday, February 24, 2016
6:09 p.m.
Javier De Leon
Will be right there. Trouble on the train.

I pick him out of the crowd that's moving north on Third Avenue. He is wearing a pin-striped coattail suit under his black leather jacket. He is much too short for a coattail suit. He gives me a crooked grin and leans in for a kiss. I jerk my face away, grab a cart and push it through the parted automatic doors. He gently takes the cart handle and walks ahead of me. I follow.

We do not speak for the 30 minutes that we walk the grocery aisles of Whole Foods. He fills the cart with tilapia, tomato sauce, spaghetti, onions, garlic, lettuce, cucumbers, lots of oranges and a package of Tates Almond Chocolate Chip cookies, his favorite. We get on line.

I stand behind him. The tension is palpable.

He turns around and studies my face. "Do you want anything else?" he asks with an awkward smile.

"Nope," I respond without looking up from my phone.

He turns back around, and I examine the specks of gray in his shiny black hair. I want to touch his hair. Being near him is intoxicating. I have known him for a little over a month and I think I am in love with this kind, doting and loving man. Until the call from my daughter yesterday morning, I was pretty sure that I had found my person. As if he read my mind, he reaches his open hand behind him, while still looking straight ahead, and I place mine in the warmth of his. I want to cry from confusion. We get to the counter, and he removes a wad of cash from his pocket and pays the cashier.

He carries all four bags the seven blocks to my apartment. We enter my apartment and I make a beeline for the bedroom, close the door and stretch across my bed. Deep inside the crevices of my being, I know that this man that I adore with such intensity after only one month is the Javier De Leon from my Google search. Tears sting the back of my eyes and drip across the bridge of my nose onto the pillow. I listen to the clanging of pots and pans in the kitchen as he prepares dinner.

I feel flutters of kisses on my face. "*Chica. Chica*, wake up. Come and get something to eat."

I open my eyes. I don't move. I look up into worried brown eyes that peer down at me in the shadows, and I am sure I love him. I am sure that I will forgive him, if it is him. He reaches for my hand, and I follow him to my tiny dining area. I look out the window to a scene that always calms me, the East River as the backdrop to headlights and taillights that create a colorful caravan along the FDR drive.

"I made tilapia, spaghetti and spinach." His voice startles me as he places a plate in front of me. I am not hungry, but I pick at it. It's bland. Across from me, he inhales his food while staring at me. Another smile creeps onto his face and just sits there. Taunting.

"What's so fucking funny, Javier?" I drop my fork, which bounces off my plate and lands with a clink on my glass table. "I can't do this eating dinner thing right now." I wave my hand and motion to the bowls of spaghetti and spinach and the baking pan with steam still rising from the fish. "Are you an ex-con or not?" I ask stiffly.

He takes our plates to the kitchen, and I listen to him scraping the food in the garbage pail.

"I just wanted to cook a nice dinner for you. That's all," he calls out dejectedly from the kitchen.

"I don't want dinner. I want to talk. Like now." I move to the couch, and he starts to wash the dishes.

"Javier! Please leave the dishes. I will take care of it. We need to talk. Now!" Anger is rising like thick smoke inside of me. With the dish towel still in his hand, he ambles over, sits next to me and takes mine. My body stiffens and my eyes fill.

"This is why I am here. I want to see your eyes and I want you to see mine when I share a chapter of my life that will haunt me for the rest of my life." He wipes a tear with the back of his hand and takes me on a journey.

Javier De Leon tells me that he was born in the Mount Hope section of the Bronx, and for as long as he can remember his mother has been addicted to drugs. A life of poverty and exposure to drug abuse was all he knew as a young boy. There were many nights that he went to bed hungry because there wasn't enough food for him and his two sisters. When he was a little boy, his uncle would sign him out of school at least twice each week and take him on long bike rides to rob houses in the affluent neighborhoods of Westchester.

"I know that you don't come from my part of the world, and this is hard for you to comprehend, but that was my reality, baby." There is sadness in his voice.

His phone pings. He scrolls through a text. "That's my son. I usually help him with his homework around now on FaceTime." He glances at his watch and returns his phone to his pocket. "Tonight, his mom will have to help him."

I stare at him blankly as he continues.

Could a man who helps his son every night with his homework be so terrible? He continues.

After he graduated from high school, he married his high-school sweetheart when they were nineteen. Fatherhood came at twenty. Widower at twenty-two, when his young wife died of ovarian cancer.

"I gave custody of my young son to my mother-in-law, because I knew that I was in no shape mentally or financially to care for him. His own grandmother, who was supposed to be a god-fearing woman, fed my child drugs so that he could appear slow for Social Security money." He removes his wallet from his back pocket and shows me photographs of a young black woman, her tombstone and finally a picture of his older son. The picture of his son is jarring. He has pointy jagged teeth and an enlarged head.

"Richard is thirty-one years old and has the mental capacity of a nine-year-old boy, all because of what his greedy grandmother did to him."

He places the pictures next to me and walks to the kitchen. He returns with two glasses of water and hands one to me. He takes a gulp, leans against the wall and continues.

"I was mad at the world after that. I didn't care what happened to me or who I hurt. I received a settlement from a car accident, bought a red Trans-Am and checked into the Parker Meridian Hotel. I thought I was hot shit! Then I loathed myself even more for wasting the money, knowing how destitute we were." He placed his face in his hands and groaned.

I study him. His story, assuming it is true, is riveting and tragic. I am sorry for his pain, but he still hasn't answered my question.

"So are you an ex-con or did you lie to me?" I scoff.

"I am an ex-con, Donna. Yes, I robbed that bank in Tamarac, Florida, decades ago. Yes, I spent seven years in federal prison and paid my debt to society. I made sure no one was hurt. I made a horrible mistake, and I regret it every day of my life.

"What do you want, a fucking medal? You swore to me that it wasn't you. And maybe you did not hurt them physically, but you still hurt them!" I scream and leap to my feet.

He grabs my arm. "Look, I regret my actions every day of my life. Knowing that I will never get a decent job. As you know, I love the stock market but will never ever get a chance to work on Wall Street. I have no one to blame but myself. In the eyes of society, I am a criminal and that is all I will ever be. But I am a good father to my sons and living my life in a way that shows them that a person can change. I am not that person anymore!" he says emphatically.

"We don't all rob banks, but everyone makes mistakes. Believe me, Javier, I have made my share of them. I get it. Yes, you made a life-altering mistake over twenty years ago—that does not make you less of a human being, and I applaud you for setting a good example for your sons. But if you continue to be deceptive, then you are still that broken human who traumatized innocent people. For money." My voice trembles as I move closer to his face with gritted teeth.

"I married two liars. If their mouths were moving, they were lying. I need someone I can finally trust, Javier. I deserve someone with integrity."

Javier being an ex-con is a lot to swallow, but I never expected him to be perfect.

Nevertheless, he had a responsibility and an obligation to tell me this not-so-small-detail, if not on day one, then soon thereafter—especially after how close we have become. I spin on my heels toward the door. I unlock it and hold it open.

"I am sorry. But I didn't want to lead with that. I wanted you to get to know me first, to see if there is any chemistry between us. I wanted you to see that I am a decent human being before dropping that on you," he pleads.

"That should have been my decision to make, not yours."

"Please give me a chance. I care deeply for you, and I know that you care for me. Please don't give up on us. What we have is too special and connected to throw away over a mistake I made decades ago." He looks at me seriously. "But I also know that if I had told you the truth over the phone yesterday morning, you would have never given me the chance to tell you my side of the story. Face to face." His pain piles up in his eyes and rolls down his face.

"Tell me something, Javier." I tilt my head to study him. "Had I not found out on my own, would you have told me?"

He grabs his jacket from the back of the recliner and shoves his arms through the leather sleeves. Silence hangs in the air.

"Are you going to answer me? Or should I assume your silence means you wouldn't have?"

"When women find out the truth about me, they discard me like trash. But I was going to tell you, after you got to know me. I am not trash, Donna. I am a human being who made a terrible mistake. I am a person!" he declares with vehemence.

"Goodnight Javier." I jerk the door wider.

"Okay," he whispers defeatedly. "I know you are upset. You have every right to be. We'll talk tomorrow?"

I look straight ahead. My tears flow freely now. My breathing constricts. He brushes a tear from my cheek with his finger, before stepping into the hallway. I slam the door behind him.

I return to the couch and wrap myself around a cushion. I smile at the irony. It has been eight years since I escaped from Jack. I used that time to focus on self-care, enjoy my passions and try to become the best possible version of myself. Yet, the first man who comes along and takes up residence in my heart, who seems like the person that I have been waiting for my whole life, is an ex-con.

Good one, universe. Good one.

Ten

GOODBYE BOOTS

I LAND IN JAMAICA on a blistering summer afternoon in August of 1974 and start my first term at Westwood High School the following month.

Mama and I arrive at Miss Birdie's house on a balmy Sunday afternoon. She lives in a nice part of Stewart Town, where Westwood is located. Everyone has phones and running water and inside toilets here like they did in New York. I am not sure how Mama knows the plump woman who opens the door, brandishing a wide smile. She motions for us to come in. We step into a grand space with a long wooden table that sits in the middle of the dining area. Above the table hangs a large black-and-white picture of someone who looks like a younger Miss Birdie, dressed in a long, flowy crinoline dress. Off to the side is a white settee with two pastel-colored pillows. The sunlight streams through the slit of a garish floral and white-laced curtain.

"Hello, Miss Neomina," Miss Birdie says to Mama. "Hello, young lady," she says to me. She wipes her round face with the back of her hand. "That will be your room over there. Go and put your suitcase down." She points to a room down the hallway.

"Thank you, Miss Birdie." I make my way down the narrow corridor and into the small room. It has a small bed, neatly made with blue-and-white-striped linen. There is a small table in the corner with a lace doily under a yellow lamp. A high-back black chair is against the wall. I plop down on the bed and survey my new living arrangements. This is where I will live for the next year because students aren't allowed to live on Westwood's campus until their second year. It is a nice, quiet room where I can focus on my studies.

I place my large suitcase stuffed with the clothes, shoes and school supplies that my mother sent in a barrel from New York on the bed, before peering through the window at the trees and a beautiful colorful garden like Mama's in the backyard. I am going to miss Mama. I amble back out to the sitting area. Mr. Junior, our cousin who was kind enough to drive the forty minutes from Duncans to Stewart Town, is leaning against the door fiddling with his cap while Mama talks quietly with Miss Birdie. They both turn to look at me, and Mama comes over.

"Do good with your book learning." Mama's face is serious as she picks up her purse from the large table and continues her lecture. "And make sure you behave yourself for Miss Birdie."

Goodbyes make me sad. "Yes, Mama." The sadness rises and sits in my chest and tears escape. I stare at the floor and bite at my nails.

"What you cryin for?" Mama asks, as I sniff and wipe my nose with the back of my hand. "You are a big girl now!"

"She gwine be alright, man. No worry," Miss Birdie assures Mama, who pats me on the back and walks out the door. Mr. Junior tilts his hat on the side of his head, waves at me and follows her.

I settle into my new life as a Westwood High School student. Each morning, I put on my navy-blue uniform, gobble down Horlicks, Milo or tea with hard-dough bread with egg or cheese, and make the walk up the steep hill to my new school that is nestled atop the mountains of Stewart Town. I fall into a routine among a sea of girls with pretty faces, fancy clothes and mothers and fathers waiting for them at home. I feel more like an outcast. I have no clue about the fashion, make-up or boyfriends that they all chatter about. I am afraid to sound stupid, so I say very little.

I push the sadness and disappointment of feeling not good enough to stay in America with my sisters and focus on my studies. In the evenings, I stay in my room and study as hard as I can. Some of my classes are English literature, Bible knowledge, arithmetic, dictation and spelling, English language, speech and drama, and piano. I look forward to Tuesday and Thursday evenings when I run track and play on the netball team, which is similar to basketball. I am spry, fast and fit. I am always in the front of the pack as we run up long hills and around the wide track. I make friends during practice. I am beginning to fit in.

I enter Miss Birdie's living room one Friday evening after school. Mr. Junior is sitting on the edge of a dining room chair, cradling his cap. I look around, but I don't see Mama. My heart drops. Something is wrong.

"Hi, Mr. Junior." I gaze at my cousin questioningly.

Miss Birdie rushes me to her bedroom at the back of the house before he can answer. "What's wrong, Miss Birdie?" I search her round face.

"Sit down, Donna." She pats the space next to her.

"Is everything alright, Miss Birdie?" My heart gallops. She pats my hand. "Your grandfather died of a heart attack on Wednesday. Mr. Junior is going to take you home to your grandmother." I stare at her, trying to process her words in my stuttering brain. I want to say something, but I can't find the words. Drops of tears fall on my shirt. She pats my hand again. Her eyes are soft. "Go and pack your bag."

It is raining during my ride back to Duncans in Mr. Junior's car. I watch the raindrops splatter against the glass and race down the windows. The car engine hums along the winding country road. I see Dada's face. His smile. His boots under the bed. His pockets bulging with sweeties. Although he is only my step-grandfather, I couldn't love him more. He can't be dead. Maybe there is some mistake.

I unlatch the large metal gate and walk toward the house. There are a lot of people on the veranda. Some are standing and others are sitting on the dining room chairs.

"Good evening," I mumble as I walk up the steps to what has been converted to a little dining area. Cooked green banana, red herring, cow-foot soup, rice and ackee and saltfish cover the table. My eyes search for Mama.

"Hello, Donna. This is my granddaughter. She go to Westwood," Mama speaks out from the corner where she is seated on a crate. She looks small and frail among the people milling about. A woman in a large straw hat hugs me. I recognize her from church. There is another woman and three men who I have seen at the market. I have no idea who the rest of these people are.

"Good evening, Mama. Good evening, everyone." They are all staring at me, which makes me somewhat self-conscious. I excuse myself and take my bag inside. During the night people come and go with food and condolences. They sing hymns, pray, and tell stories about Dada.

Mama tells the story repeatedly: "Dada wasn't feeling well in his body. It took him almost two hours to walk to Dr. Foote's office, a walk that would normally take fifteen minutes. It took him even longer to come back. When he got to the front gate his heart just give out and him drop down dead in the hot sun at exactly one o'clock in the afternoon."

I gaze at Dada's black boots in their usual spot under the bed before picking them up and holding them against my chest. Dada loved these boots. I think of the morning he placed his foot in one that was filled with pee, because I mistook it for the chamber pot in the middle of the night. I remember how he laughed as he removed his wet sock. I can still see him on the top veranda step, his back and arms moving wildly, as he cleaned and polished them until they almost sparkled. Dada is the closest I have ever come to having a father. I sit in the darkness and my tears fall on his big boots. I climb into the bed of my childhood and lie in the middle and imagine that Mama and Dada are on either side of me. The way we used to sleep each night, because I thought duppies were in the other room. The chatter and singing of the mourners on the veranda buzz about in my head. I fall asleep cradling big black boots.

Two days later, I sit on the bottom step and watch the people in black surround the high mound of fresh dirt in the cemetery down the hill. I tug at my black dress and wait patiently for Mama to come out of the house. She doesn't, but I hear her. What Mama is doing is more than crying. It is a wretched scream that comes from a person who has lost it all. Mama is stretched out across the bed, her neatly pressed black dress laid out next to her. I sit on the edge of the bed.

"Mama, they are waiting for us to come down," I whisper.

"Me not going. Me not going!" she wails.

Several people come up to the house, but Mama refuses to leave the bed. The funeral starts and I can hear the singing and the preaching. I want to go to say goodbye to Dada, but I don't want to leave Mama like this. Suddenly, she gets up and walks zombie-like through the door, leaving her black dress untouched. We walk in silence down the hill and stand side-by-side, Mama still in her regular house dress, as Dada's shiny coffin is placed in the brown earth.

Mama's knees buckle and people hold her up as she says goodbye to her husband underneath the blistering sun.

I return to Westwood after Dada's funeral and continue my quest to be liked and accepted. I had always thought of myself as a good student who received decent grades and positive feedback from my teachers. Why wouldn't that have been the case? After all, I was accepted into one of the most prestigious high schools in Jamaica and clearly this confirmed my intelligence and potential.

I thought this until recently, when I stumbled upon an actual Westwood report card from 1974. I studied the decades-old, yellowed, creased, and lined parchment-style paper with the blue-inked cursive handwriting styles of my twelve teachers. Strong symmetrical lines, different-sized letters, teeny scrawls, and large rounded letters. I gazed at the different comments, which told a different story.

Donna must work more steadily. Donna is lazy and does little work. Donna needs to be more attentive. Donna tries hard.

Donna must put more concentrated effort into all her work.

Donna is a quiet member of the form. She needs to participate more in form and school affairs.

I ranked thirty-first of a class of thirty-five. In retrospect, I wonder if perhaps being taken from the only home I knew, being betrayed by my best friend Naomi and a life of feeling abandoned by grownups, was hitting me harder than I realized.

* * *

My mother invites me back to New York and my summer break of 1975 in East Flatbush, Brooklyn, is just as delightful as the year before.

I am finally living on-campus as a true Westwoodite. Westwood is like an all-girls finishing and military school combined. On one hand we are taught the finer social graces and etiquette that are to prepare us to enter society with a certain refinement. So instead of inhaling and slurping my meals as I am used to doing at Mama's large wooden table, I now focus on table settings, making sure that I am at least two hand-widths away from the table, and that my elbows never come in contact with it. My knees and ankles must never be apart, and I must dab, not wipe, the corners of my mouth before daintily and carefully returning the cloth napkin to my lap. What is probably the most challenging is the placement of food on the back of the fork.

Oh, yeah. And cursing is reserved for hooligans.

The boarding school system is heavily structured, and the school is run by bells that dole out fractions of the day in chunks. Wake up. Dining room. Devotion. Classes. Study session. Extracurricular activities. Shower. Lights out. There is even a bell to go to church. Each Sunday morning, it chimes, and we line up in pairs for the organized walk down the steep hill, through the town toward the Anglican Church.

The townsfolk peer from their windows or gawk from the sidewalks or their cars as we file past. Westwood is a highly respected school, and I am proud to stand among this sea of girls as we meander through the parish, dressed in our signature navy-blue tunics, white shirts, navy-blue socks, black penny-loafers and straw hats encircled with navy-blue ribbons.

Except for the weekends and holidays, we don't have a lot of free time. Our schedules are jam-packed with classes, study sessions and sports. So, I am beyond excited when it is announced that we are going on a class trip to Dunns River Falls in Ocho Rios. I have heard people talk about the falls, a popular tourist attraction with a giant cascading waterfall on the northern coast of the island and have always wanted to go.

On the morning of the trip, I am much too excited to sleep. While my dorm mates are still asleep, I quietly climb off my top bunk and put on my eggshell-colored two-piece bathing suit with the scalloped edges, which my mother bought for me while I was in New York. I pull my sundress over it and sit in the lounge, brimming with excited impatience, waiting for the "wake up" bell to ring, so that we can have breakfast and be on our way to the falls. In a few hours the large bus is filled with the chatter of young schoolgirls as it trundles through the countryside toward Dunns River Falls.

It is even more majestic and magical than I could have imagined. We spend the day frolicking and giggling with delight, as we push against the cool water flow to climb the rugged and slippery terrain. After we reach the top, we hurry to the bottom to form another human chain and climb up again and again, until it is time to return to campus. One of the best days of my twelve-year-old-life. On our way back, I stare out the bus window and study the sunset as rich hues of orange and red splatter across the horizon. Some girls are sleeping. Some are chatting, their voices blending and rising. I am lost in my own thoughts as I replay the day in my mind like a movie reel. The powerful water gushing down against the white rocks over us. Our squeals. Our laughter. Such sweet fun. Aside from my time in New York City, this is one of the best days of my life. Yet, the ache of longing to be with my mother and sisters is trapped in my bones. I wish more than anything that I could have shared this day with them.

* * *

It's a Friday morning in the spring of 1976, weeks before my fourteenth birthday. I am standing on the line in the dining hall for mid-morning snack. Today it is jelly between crackers. One step. My stomach growls and I count the number of girls ahead of me. Eight. Two more steps. I glance at the clock and wonder if it is broken. One more step. The closer I get, the longer it seems to take each girl to take two cracker sandwiches and a cup of red juice. I see my friend Wilma standing off to the side, gesturing and mouthing something to me, but I can't understand her, and I don't want to lose my place in the line. Wilma is one of the prettiest and most popular girls in school and sometimes I find it hard to believe that we are friends. I feel a sense of pride when we walk around campus together.

I am finally at the front of the line.

"Take only two," the lunch lady with the hairnet cautions as she hands me a cup of the red liquid. I finish the crumbly crackers with jelly with two bites, gulp down the fruity drink and amble over to Wilma.

"What?" I ask, and dump the plastic cup in the large garbage container. "Look how much they have left over? I'm still hungry!"

She points to the table with the leftover crackers.

"So? You know we can't have any more!" I remind her.

"As soon as the bell rings, let's grab some when they are not looking!" Wilma surveys the room.

"I'm hungry, too. But I don't think we should," I caution, secretly worrying that I am annoying my popular friend with my cowardice.

The bell rings and the girls begin to file out of the dining room. Wilma pulls me behind the door.

"Why not? You 'fraid?" Wilma whispers and points at me accusingly.

"I don't want to get into trouble!"

"Stop being so 'fraidy 'fraidy fool fool pickney!" She chants and laughs mockingly.

"I am not 'fraidy 'fraidy!" I shoot back, trying to sound brave.

I study her perfect olive skin and curly black hair. Wilma is smiling at me. Daring me. I peek out from behind the door. The dining hall is almost empty, and the hairnet women are busily distracted, wiping down the counters. The left-over crackers are scattered across a large silver tray only a few feet away.

"Okay, but we must hurry. We can't get caught!" I say, smiling back at her. My heart is jackhammering in my chest. I do not want to do this, but I also don't want her to stop being my friend. Suddenly, Wilma pushes me toward the tray and for a split second I change my mind, but there's no turning back.

We both grab a handful and stuff them in our pockets and rush toward the large brown double doors.

"Stop right there!" We turn to face Miss Geraldine, the white assistant principal who is also my piano teacher. I feel the blood drain from my face. Miss Geraldine is the meanest teacher at Westwood. She walks with a stoop, and she never smiles. Her gray hair is pulled into a tight bun, which accentuates her blue eyes and severe scowl.

"What did you just put in your pockets?" I turn to look at Wilma who is picking something from under her nails.

"What did you just put in your pockets? Answer me when I ask you a question!" Her voice fills the now empty dining hall, except for a few students who are now staring.

"We were still hungry, so we take extra crackers." My voice shakes.

"It's we took extra crackers. Took, not take!" she barks. "Meet me in my office at the end of your classes." Ms. Geraldine walks off toward the study hall.

A small group is gathering. Some are pointing and laughing. I roll my eyes and push past Wilma and head toward my next class.

I knock on Miss Geraldine's office door at 3 p.m. I hear her footsteps on the other side before she opens the door and ushers me in. Miss Geraldine's office is a large room that

overlooks the hill. Piles and piles of sheet music and paper
cover chairs, the floor and her desk.

"Take a seat." She points to the only uncluttered chair. I
take a seat. Her blue eyes dig into me. She clears her throat
but takes forever to speak. I am pretty sure that they are going to throw me out of Westwood. I try to stop myself from
shaking by counting.

One. Two. Three. Four.

"Young lady, what you did today is a violation, and you
are being assigned a B-Order Mark. We will not tolerate such
hoggish behavior in this school. Do you understand me?" She
narrows her freakishly blue eyes and glares at me.

"Yes, Miss Geraldine. But I was—"

"No buts. Rules are rules." She interrupts. I study her
pale face and for the first time I notice the wrinkled grooves
around her mouth and the wavy pattern of her hair. "You
are to wear your uniform over the weekend and scrub all the
toilets on the lower level."

There are three disciplinary marks at Westwood: A, B
and C Order Marks. The A is reserved for the most egregious
offenses and the B falls somewhere in the middle. I am no
longer listening as I watch her ugly wrinkled mouth. I have
been a model student for the past year and a half. Never once
in trouble. But I guess that means nothing to her. I bite my
bottom lip and try not to cry, but by the time her mouth stops
moving, the tears have escaped and dampened the white collar of my uniform. A small part of me is filled with indigna-
tion about being punished. There were plenty of crackers left
over, and I was hungry! She opens the door and ushers me
out. Wilma is waiting. I look at her, but she ignores me, pushes past and slams the door behind her.

I spend the weekend in full uniform on my knees. Under the watchful eye of a prefect, I move from toilet to toilet

scrubbing the smelly porcelain, grimy hand basins and dusty tiles. Girls prance around in their bell bottom pants, colorful shirts, dresses and platform shoes. They look at me knowingly. That is the whole point of the uniform during the weekends, the only time we are allowed to wear casual clothes. So that everyone will know that I am in trouble.

I am released at dusk. My knees, back and hands ache from the vigorous scrubbing, and exhaustion makes my body hang like a wet noodle. I sit on the stairs near the study hall and watch the orange sun set in the sky. Bold and bright as the oranges that fall from Mama's tree. I sit in the silence feeling sorry for myself. Dada is dead. Wilma probably won't be my friend anymore. My mother and sisters are a world away. I don't think my father cares if I live or die. The day Sherlock and my sisters left abruptly and without me, won't stop playing like a movie reel in my head. It is almost dark before I make my way along the stony path to my dorm room, feeling once again like a stray dog.

* * *

Mr. Junior pulls up to the side of the road that leads to Mama's house, and I lug my suitcase up the hill to start my summer vacation. I glance over at Dada's tombstone.

"Hi Dada," I whisper, and a feeling of sadness covers me.

Mama is waiting for me at the gate. "You look like big woman. Look pon you fat batty!" Mama pats my butt, throws her head back and laughs.

"Good afternoon, Mama." I giggle at her silliness, self-consciously aware that my body is changing. Lion and Jane Grip surround me with hello barks and wagging tails as I walk across the veranda and into the extra room. I plop down on the bed and look around. It feels different now that Dada is gone.

"Me make some ackee and saltfish. Come eat something."
Mama motions for me to follow her to the kitchen. With
Dada gone, I can only imagine how lonely Mama must be.

"How are you, Mama?" I ask, studying her face.

"Lawd, what a way you speaky-spokey now that you get
book learning. How old you are now? Me forget."

"I just turned fourteen, Mama," I reply and chomp on a
piece of dumpling. She places a piece of cassava pudding on
the table, and I can't wait to taste it. I wish I could eat Mama's cooking every day. I can eat as much as I want, and I
don't have to clean toilets because I took too much. I push the
memory from my mind.

"Thanks, Mama." My eyes follow her as she cleans the
stove. I wait a few anxious minutes. "Have you heard from
my mother?"

It takes a while for her to answer.

"You are not going back to Westwood. Your mother send
for you. You moving to America."

I stare at her back. I want to jump on her large wooden
table and scream. I have waited my whole life to hear those
words. I contain my excitement and honor the heaviness in
Mama's voice, even though my insides are screaming with joy.

"Mama, maybe you should come too," I suggest, knowing
that she has sworn never to get on a plane.

"If God wanted me to fly, him woulda give me wings." She
glances back at me with a quick laugh as she walks out the
door with the leftovers for the dogs.

Soon enough we cruise along the winding road toward
Sangster International Airport. From the back seat, I stare
at the back of the yellow-checkered scarf that wraps around
Mama's head. She looks straight ahead. Unspoken feelings of
sadness ball up in my chest as Mr. Junior's car moves along
the road. My mind rushes back to last night as we stuffed my

suitcase with mangoes, tamarind, and bulla and cheese.

"Never forget that you are a child of God. Do good and he will always take care of you."

"Yes, Mama."

"You drop and hit your head in the school yard and almost bleed to death. People tried to kill you with Obeah, and the plane almost crash and kill you two years ago. But you still here because God has a plan for your life." She whispers something almost inaudible as if praying, before continuing. "Get your book learning and do what God says and he will bless you with a wonderful life."

"I will, Mama."

We arrive at the airport, and she gives me another lecture, this time with tears brimming. "Do well with your studies."

"Yes, Mama." I smile at her trying not to cry as I hug her, breathing in her sweet familiar smell of curry and thyme.

"Make sure you write me." Her smile is weak.

"I will, Mama." I give her one last hug and head down the corridor.

The plane taxis down the runway toward my brand-new life in America. I stare out the small window, and warm tears crawl down my face. I know that Mama is somewhere in the airport watching the plane take off as the ground falls away. I wave at no one in particular.

Eleven

VALLEY OF THE SHADOW

1976

MY FIRST EVENING AS A NEW YORKER is spent under a canvas roof revival tent on Hopkinson Avenue in Brooklyn. The July heat is suffocating. People are settled in rows and rows of metal chairs above a sawdust floor, some fanning themselves furiously with paper fans. The preacher jumps and stomps across the pulpit.

"Hallelujah-hah! Thank you Jeeeeesus-hah!"

A portly man plays the organ, his hands climbing up and down the scales. People clap, bang on tambourines, sing and holy-ghost dance with such intensity that a sawdust fog covers us like a thin veil. A man takes off running, circling the perimeter of the tent, flailing his arms. I stifle a laugh. Services at the little church in Duncans were much more dignified. I don't remember people running wildly or falling down trembling in the aisles. It's as if they are under some sort of spell. We go every night.

On the seventh evening, a force pulls me to the front of the tent during the altar call. I raise my hands and a brown-skinned young woman wraps her arms around my shoulders and prays with me. For about thirty minutes, I tearfully ask God to free me from the painful childhood memories and emotional wounds that I carry in my chest. To help me to forgive. To surrender my life to his care. I take a vow to live the rest of my life as a born- again-Christian on a sweltering Friday evening in July of 1976. I am fourteen years old.

She asks me to repeat the Sinners Prayer.

Dear God. I am a sinner
and I ask for forgiveness of all my sins.

Come into my heart and guide my life
and help me to do your will.

I accept you as my personal savior.

In Jesus' name.

Amen.

"Amen."

I leave the dusty tent feeling a peace like nothing I have ever felt before.

Samuel J. Tilden High School is a world away from the hills of Westwood. On my first day, I stand to the side and watch the students move along the shiny hallway. Teachers hurry by. A cacophony of wild teenage chatter and raucous laughter fill the space against a colorful backdrop of bell-bottoms, frayed jeans, short-shorts, ankle-length maxi dresses, Adidas sneakers and platform shoes. Pretty girls with shiny bouncy curls, afro-framed faces and shiny lips, giggle with each other or hang on the words of muscled jocks. That familiar outcast feeling fills me.

Because of church, I am not allowed to wear make-up or

fancy clothes—not that I have any. I must remain prayerful at all times as a new convert. I make it through all my classes that first day in shock at the way the students behave. They throw things, pop gum, cuss and talk back to the teacher like wild hooligans. I didn't expect Westwood, but I certainly didn't expect this. It is all a little unsettling and I am happy that my older sister Grace is also a student here. I make it to my sophomore year, still adjusting to my American school.

"Donna Pinnock." The homeroom teacher is taking attendance the first day after summer break.

"Present." My voice shakes.

"Look at her face. Damn!" Jenny nudges one of her friends and points at me. "She needs some Ambi!" She throws her head back and laughs at the eruption of acne and scars that now cover my fifteen-year-old face. "From now on, her new name will be Ambi!" she giggles, and looks in my direction.

I stare at the floor and try not to react to being called by the name of a skin-bleaching cream. Jenny is about six-feet tall, with coal-colored skin and reminds me of a linebacker. Four other girls are always with her, hanging on her every word and laughing at her jokes. Jenny is the class bully who chose me as her target about a month into my freshman year.

Even though I sat quietly each day at the back of the homeroom class, desperate to be inconspicuous and praying that she forgot that I existed, her eyes scanned the room until they found me. I tensed, knowing that for the next hour crumpled paper would be tossed, insults about my face would be hurled, and everyone in the room would laugh and point. Even more infuriating, the homeroom teacher would ignore it all. I made it through my first year of homeroom praying for my enemies and reading my Bible as I am taught to do.

Here I sit, one year later. My prayers clearly failed to work because Jenny is back at it and practically everyone in the room is doubled over with laughter at my expense, yet again.

"Quiet down," the homeroom teacher shouts. They ignore him.

I watch their laughing faces; a ball of sweltering humiliation fills me.

"What you looking at, Ambi?" Jenny barks, and glares at me.

I look away and try to convince myself that I don't care. The bell rings and I rush through the back door, but Jenny and her friends follow me. My heart hammers against my chest. They circle me in the hallway. Some students stop to watch the commotion, while others seem disinterested as they meander through the small crowd that is starting to form around us.

"Why do you have so many bumps on your face, Ambi?" Jenny pushes me and my back bounces against the blue-gray lockers that line the shiny hallway.

The LORD is my shepherd; I shall not want.

"Answer me, Ambi!" She pushes me again.

He makes me lie down in green pastures. He leads me beside still waters.

One of her friends' bookbag connects with my back. I stumble forward.

He restoreth my soul. He leads me in paths of righteousness for his name's sake.

I study the faces of the students around me. Some are laughing, others are clapping, but no one is trying to help me.

Even though I walk through the valley of the shadow of death, I will fear no evil.

I am back in the dining hall in Westwood. Miss Geraldine is in my face. Girls are pointing and laughing. Hot rage twirls around inside my throat. In Westwood, I was taught that fighting is reserved for unladylike hooligans. In church, I am taught to turn the other cheek. I don't want to be a lady right now and turning the other cheek seems stupid. I reach back and smack Jenny across the face as hard as I can. *Whack!*

I can't believe I just did that.

"Fight! Fight!" Some students yell. Others bounce up and down with excitement like idiot rabbits.

She lunges at me. I dodge and push through the crowd, run down the hallway and into my English class. Teachers and students look around suspiciously. I hear footsteps behind me. My chest is beginning to burn.

For thou art with me, thy rod and thy staff, they comfort me.

I run to the back of the room and wedge myself into a corner. Jenny lunges at me. Misses.

"Get out of here now!" My English teacher's voice fills the room. They ignore her.

I can't find my breath.

"I said now. And I mean right now! Get! Out!" She barks and points her arm to the open door, where students have gathered to watch the commotion.

"I will see you after school, Ambi!" Jenny makes a fist at me before retreating. I watch her big linebacker back through angry tears.

My English teacher instructs me to follow her and we hurry along the hallway and down the stairs to the first floor. She tells my guidance counselor what just happened and leaves. I am sobbing hard. He reaches in his briefcase and hands me a piece of tissue and motions for me to sit. His voice is gentle.

"These girls are bullies, and I would just stay away from them if I were you." He scans a list and continues. "The only class that you have with them is homeroom. So, going forward, don't go to homeroom, come here to my office and I will take your attendance. Stay out of their way in the hallways and don't walk alone after school. These girls are bad news!"

He makes notes in a little brown notebook. I wait for him to say that they will be reported to the principal. Suffer some sort of consequence. Anything, but stay out of their way. Essentially, they can continue being hooligans for as long as they want.

At 3 p.m. I exit the building and scan the mass of students, sick of being afraid but relieved that Jenny and her crew are nowhere in sight. My face splits into a grin at the sight of my sister, who is leaning against the railing, her long legs out-stretched as her eyes roam over the crowd. I hurry over to her, so happy that she is still here, even though her classes ended an hour earlier.

"Thanks for waiting for me. Did you hear what hap-pened?" I ask as we hurry down the stairs.

"Yes. I heard. That's why I waited." She grins. Grace has always had a calming effect on me. I grin back. As we stand at the corner waiting for the light to change, I look over at my sister and couldn't love her more.

The following day, instead of going to homeroom, I enter my guidance counselor's office, to begin a daily routine that would last for the rest of the semester. I sit in the chair outside his office and watch the students move along the hallway in groups, their sounds of laughter and excited chatter filling the space. My sister and a couple of my friends stop by from time to time to check in on me before going to their homeroom.

I assure them that I am alright, but I am really not. Sitting here under the harsh ceiling lights that illuminate my guid-ance counselor's windowless office, I can't help but feel like a cowardly outcast. Alone in a building full of people. I wish I had the courage to storm into my homeroom class and stand up to those five girls. But I know I don't.

So I read my Bible and try to push down the familiar feel-ings of isolation. Feelings akin to being on my knees cleaning toilets at Westwood or snuggled alone in the corner of the red veranda. An outcast.

Twelve

THEY CALL ME BETTY HILL

1982

I WATCH HIM FROM THE FRONT ROW of the choir. He enters the sanctuary with a marching walk. Deliberate steps with shoulders back as if he is a soldier in the army. He is stylishly dressed in a crisp blue suit with a coordinated tie and pocket handkerchief.

Except for the occasional 'Praise the Lord' in passing, I have never really spoken to Michael Cowers, but have certainly admired him from afar.

When the church announces that they will be putting on its first theatrical production, I decide to audition. I am nineteen years old and studying theatre and communications at Hunter College in New York City. The play is called *The Son of Man,* scribed by one of the elders. On audition day, I enter the church and a small group is seated in the two front pews. I sit two rows behind them. I immediately notice Michael and I am very happy that he is here. I take the stage nervously and recite the audition piece of First Corinthians 13. I am cast as Betty Hill, the lead character and a troubled teenager. Michael is hired as a lighting technician.

I had always known I wanted to be an actress since the first night Mama and I watched the little black-and-white television with the American shows. I was drawn to the idea of becoming someone else and losing myself in the feelings and thoughts of another. Aside from singing to the chickens, the dogs and Mama's flowers, tonight is the first time I will perform in front of a real audience.

I stand at the back of the church waiting to make my entrance. The lights dim, the director pulls the doors open and adrenaline pumps violently through my body. With a red bandana wrapped around my head and a large boom box balancing on my shoulder, I make my way down the aisle toward the dimly lit stage. All eyes are on me. You can hear a pin drop and my heart beats in my ears. For the next two and a half hours, I am not Donna from Duncans, I am Betty Hill, a wounded and aggressive teenager who hates everyone and everything. I breathe life into her, and she breathes life into me. I float around on a cloud of euphoria and intensity until the last scene, when I fall at Jesus' feet and beg tearfully for forgiveness as the choir sings the closing number. The audience jumps to its feet and goes wild for seven straight nights. I have found a new home on the stage.

We close on a Thursday night. I take my bow and head backstage. I can't seem to turn off my character, Betty Hill, and the parade of emotions that are still marching through my body from embodying her. My sadness and her sadness blend and I sob into my hands, stopping only to refill my lungs and continue.

"Are you okay?" Michael's voice startles me. He is standing across the hallway, studying me.

"What are you doing back here? You scared me."

I feel disoriented as I wipe my face with the back of my

hand. I have never really talked privately with boys before, outside of family members. During high school, I was practically invisible to them, which was for the better, because having a boyfriend was not allowed. Even now at the age at nineteen, no one has explicitly sought me out and I continue to feel awkward and shy in the presence of the opposite sex. My face feels hot with embarrassment about the hysterics that Michael just witnessed.

"I am just putting away some of the cables." He points to a large plastic container. "What's wrong?"

"Nothing. I'm fine." I wipe at tears that won't stop coming.

"Here, take this." He hands me his handkerchief with a sheepish grin.

"Thank you." I dab my face. "I have to go and change for the meet and greet. Thanks."

I stand and hand him his handkerchief. Our hands touch. Linger. The room is warm. He pulls me close to him and wraps me in a hug and I hug him back. The smell of his Grey Flannel cologne invades my nostrils and time stands still for what feels like an hour. Then it ends as abruptly as it began. We pull apart awkwardly and he heads down the stairs and up the aisle toward the back of the church. Although I was just hugged by a strange man, it was nevertheless a hug from gentle arms. I don't get many of those.

I hurry to the dressing room with a smile plastered across my face.

He sits next to me during the cast dinner, but we do not speak of the stolen hug. I catch him staring at me a few times and I stare back when he's not looking. I am drawn to his dark features. Neat wavy hair, overly thick eyebrows and dark almond-shaped eyes. I love being this close to him, but getting to know him is not an option. Our lives must be focused on praying, and Jesus' love and plan for our lives.

Fun activities are forbidden in our church: movies, sports, television and dating are reserved for sinners. Women aren't allowed to wear make-up or pants, cut our hair or shave. Marriages are arranged between the Pastor and God.

Nevertheless, we always find a way to talk to each other and hang on each other's words with gazes that linger way too long, after which my heart somersaults with such intensity that I swear everyone can hear its thumping as butterflies, very large ones, dance around in my stomach. There is just something about the way Michael laughs that makes my soul smile. I find comfort in the softness of his dark brown eyes. Eventually, we admit to ourselves and to each other what we have known all along, but were too terrified to do because of the restrictions. We are in love. For the next year, Michael and I call each other from random payphones. We meet secretly at restaurants and take walks in Central Park and the Bronx Zoo, engrossed in the tales of each other's lives. He tells me that he has a five-year-old daughter and shows me a picture of a beautiful little mixed-race girl with a head full of curls and a wide smile. She is sitting on the lap of her mother, who appears to be Asian.

As I stare at the picture, I am shocked that a nineteen-year-old has a five-year-old, but I don't allow the shock to register on my face.

"That's my little pumpkin, Ella." He beams proudly and returns the picture to his wallet.

"Isn't it hard being a father so young?" I ask, studying his face.

"It is, but my ex-girlfriend lives with her parents, and they help us. A lot."

"Oh. I see." I don't know what to say.

"I have turned my life over to the Lord and I plan to live for him for the rest of my days." He wants to be a minister and get his seven siblings and his mother to turn their lives over to the Lord. He wants to be a minister. I like that.

I tell him about the father I don't really know, my child-hood in Jamaica, my strained relationship with my mother and my hopes and dreams of becoming a performer. I love his sense of humor, gentle sweet disposition and chivalrous gestures, such as opening doors for me and insisting that I walk on the inside of the sidewalk. I feel safer with him than I have ever felt with another person.

It is a Thursday evening in the early spring of 1983. Michael hands me a small white box as we walk south on Lexington Avenue after my evening class at Hunter College. My hands shake as I open it and stare wide-eyed at the two wedding bands and an engagement ring with a tiny diamond.

"Let's get married!" he proposes.

"The Pastor has to give his blessing, and who knows what my mother will do," I remind him, searching his face.

"We should at least try. There is no other way for us to be together. And I love you." His voice cracks. My heart is racing. I have no words as I cradle the small white box. I want to be with him more than anything.

"I am scared of your mother, though." We both laugh nervously.

"I love you too, Michael." I look up at his face as we stand in the bustle of Lexington Avenue. I wish we were allowed to kiss. "I will tell her tomorrow." I try to sound calm.

I time it perfectly and tell her just as she is about to walk out the door the following Friday evening.

"Mommy, Michael gave me a ring." I keep the small white box behind me and stare nervously at the word "Welcome" on the door mat. She doesn't acknowledge me. She grabs her coat, keys and Bible and pushes past me to open the door. She stops suddenly as if hearing my words for the first time, and spins around to face me.

The blood drains from my face as her eyes settle briefly on mine.

"Oh, yeah?" She scans me up and down before stepping

into the hallway and slamming the door behind her.

The next day is a typical Saturday, and my Mother says nothing about the ring. She is unusually quiet. We do our chores in silence. She makes "Saturday soup" as we call it, with more vegetables than we care for. Her sewing machine whirs as she stitches her new dress for tomorrow's service. Every now and then, I feel her eyes on me. I don't make eye contact with her. While brushing my teeth that night, she enters the bathroom and stands behind me. She studies my reflection quietly as she ties a yellow and beige scarf around her head. Being near my mother now, I realize that she is just as much a stranger as she was when she visited me in Duncans during my childhood. I focus on the water sputtering from the faucet.

"The Pastor wants to see you tomorrow before the morning service." I look up to catch her subtle grin as she leaves the bathroom. I want to ask why. But I don't dare. I rinse my mouth and turn off the lights and climb into bed beside my sister.

I am ushered into the Pastor's study by one of the church ladies. I am wearing my black-and-white choir robe and my small-stone engagement ring. I take a seat and look around his office and wait for him to finish a phone call. He sits behind a huge, shiny and brown mahogany desk. The writing tools are equally shiny. A grand picture of him hangs on the wall high above his desk. In it, he holds a giant burgundy Bible above his head and looks toward the sky. The carpeting is paisley gray and there are two huge vases brimming with long-stemmed silk flowers. I am not aware that he ended his call and is watching me. I meet his squinted eyes and feel the fear crawl up my throat. This is the powerful pastor of a 5,000-person congregation.

My mother worships him. He banishes people to the upper level of our theater-turned-church if they sin—for the purpose of deterrence and public humiliation. He sighs and folds his hands together on his desk.

"Why are you disrespecting your mother's house with that young man?" he asks sternly.

"I am not and have never disrespected my mother's house, Pastor," I object weakly.

"She is a woman of God!" he snaps back accusingly.

"I am not sure what you heard, but—"

"Take that ring off your finger!" he cuts me off. "You are never to see him again. Jesus is coming back soon, and you need to get your house in order." He moves from behind his desk and stands directly in front of me.

"But I didn't do anything wrong," I protest feebly.

The Bible encourages marriage, so I don't understand what I have done wrong. I fell in love and got engaged to someone from the church. I am in my second year of college. I obey the word of God. I fast. I pray. I preach on the buses and hand out tracts in Time Square. Why is he treating me like a criminal? Is something wrong with Michael? Is it because Michael has a five- year-old at nineteen years old?

"This conversation is over. Take that ring off in the name of Jesus!" He points at my hand and glares through the heavy silence. After a seemingly long pause, I slowly remove the ring and hold it in my clenched fist. I feel the angry tears burning the backs of my eyes but refuse to release them.

"I have to get ready for service," he says and returns behind his desk.

And just like that, the conversation is over. The church lady opens the door and pokes her head in as if she has been listening. We walk in silence up the staircase to the door that leads to the choir's entrance. She hovers briefly, and then turns and hurries down the stairs that lead back to the Pastor's study. I watch the back of her white silken head cover as she closes the door behind her.

The tears flow freely now. I wipe my face and shove my engagement ring back onto my finger and move past the choir entrance, down the long corridor toward the carpeted stairs that lead to the basement where Michael waits. We push the large red-and-gold ornate doors open and step into the hustle and bustle of Jamaica Avenue. I can hear the choir that I have been a member for the past seven years, singing in the background, but I don't look back. The Q56 bus shuttles us from Queens to my mother's apartment in Flatbush, Brooklyn where I pack my clothes and leave her keys with a neighbor. I look behind me as the taxi moves along the tree-lined street of Ocean Avenue and take a deep breath, allowing the relief to flow through me.

Michael and I hold hands for the first time.

After the pastor ordered me to remove my engagement ring from my finger and never see Michael again, we knew that we had to leave the church, a place that has been my life for the past seven years. I will miss my sisters, my friends, church services, singing in the choir and performing in the church's drama club. I rest my head against his shoulder as the taxi cruises toward the East New York section of Brooklyn.

My new best friend Ann, who I met when we both performed in the play, had offered to let me stay with her until we get married.

Thirteen

NIGHT CRAWLERS

SIX DAYS LATER, ON FRIDAY, May 20, 1983, I don my wedding gown, a white high-necked, long-sleeved cotton dress that I found on a sale rack at Macy's. It is raining buckets. In some cultures, there is a belief that rain on your wedding day means good luck. Ann and I take the long train ride from her mother's apartment to the East Tremont section of the Bronx. We meet Michael, his mother and sister at Michael's father's apartment, a fifth-floor walkup in a semi-abandoned building overlooking the Bronx Zoo. My eyes are drawn to a dying cockroach quivering on its back in the corner of the living room.

On the train ride to City Hall, I study my groom. He looks particularly handsome in his navy-blue suit and light blue tie. The do-rag-induced waves in his hair accentuate his long lashes and beautiful dark brown eyes. I adore this man and can't wait to start our lives together. I think of Mama and Dada. Even as a little girl, I knew that they loved each other. There was something in the way his eyes would light up when she entered the room, how she smiled at him when she placed his food in front of him and the extra tenderness they showed after they argued. I want that for us.

We hold hands, repeat our vows, exchange rings and kiss. It is quicker than I expected, and within a few minutes, after instructing us not to throw rice, the judge announces my new name: Mrs. Michael Cowers. It is still raining when we leave the courthouse.

My first year of marriage is wedded bliss. I enter a new and unfamiliar world of a "sinner." He takes me dancing, to movies and amusement parks. I wear slacks and makeup without fear of someone seeing me and reporting back to the church. I watch television shows that I did not know existed and listen to music that I was only vaguely familiar with. Michael records a mixtape for me. I listen to Teddy Pendergrass, Lionel Richie, Roberta Flack, Luther Vandross, Barry White and Marvin Gaye over and over again, music that I was told would secure my place in hell. Michael works as a bank teller for Citibank, and I enter my junior year at Hunter College, studying Theatre and Mass Communications. But we can't make ends meet because his salary is barely enough to cover rent and basic expenses. Our only furniture is a platform bed, which Michael bought just before we got married, and two used dressers.

Our refrigerator doesn't work, so we keep milk and juice on the windowsill during the winter. We don't have much, but we have each other.

It's a Friday evening and a few days before our first wedding anniversary. I cash my check from my new temp job as a receptionist and decide to ditch class to spend the evening with my husband. I stop by the local Chinese restaurant in our Bronx neighborhood and pick up Michael's favorite: sweet and sour chicken, fried rice, a side order of chicken wings with extra soy sauce.

The light is on in our bedroom when I get home.

"Michael, I have a surprise for you," I call out from the kitchen and place the bags on the counter. Silence. "Michael! Where are you?" Nothing. "Babe?"

"I'm in here," he calls from our bedroom.

"Baby didn't you hear me call...?" I freeze at the doorway. Michael is leaning against the wall. "This is my friend, Andrea, from the bank. She just stopped by to drop off some paperwork." Michael walks toward me and wraps an arm around my shoulder. "Andrea, this is my wife, Donna."

She gives me a weak smile from the edge of the bed where she sits, dressed in tight blue jeans and a pink floral shirt. Her long black hair is pulled into a neat ponytail that cascades in layers down her back. A pink leather jacket and a black pocketbook are beside her.

"I'm sorry, who are you?" I asked, trying to contain my burning rage.

"Hi, Donna. I'm Andrea. Nice to meet you. I was just leaving." She stands and grabs her bag and jacket.

"Good. Because I am about to have dinner with my husband," I shoot back, and spin around toward the kitchen to fix our plates. My blood boils. My hands shake. Michael is my family. My home. I don't have anyone else. The thought of him having an affair makes me feel as if I am gasping for air. I glance at them from the kitchen as he ushers her down the hallway to the front door. The door locks and I hear his footsteps approaching.

"How was your day, baby?" He appears in the doorway with his usual silly smile.

"So are you going to tell me who that was and why she was sitting on our bed?" I glare at him.

"I told you already, baby. That was my co-worker. She dropped off some information that I need." He waves his hand dismissively. "Please don't make a big deal over nothing."

"Then why didn't she just hand it to you at the door?" I walk toward him, fire burning in my face. "Why was she sitting on our bed, Michael?"

"We don't have any furniture. Where else would she sit, babe? Plus, she was doing me a favor, I just wanted to show her our new place." He grabs a chicken wing from the white take-out container. "Go get comfortable and relax, I'll finish fixing our plates." He grins at me and takes a greasy bite.

Michael and I sit above our TV trays and eat greasy Chinese food. *Wheel of Fortune* is on. I laugh with him as we try to out-solve each other. I try to dismiss the uneasiness that is swirling around in the deepest crevices of my belly. I don't say anything else, because I need my husband to love me forever.

Over the next few months, Michael changes drastically, and I no longer recognize my husband. He's rude and distant. He comes home late or disappears in the middle of the night while I am asleep. His "I went to see my friends" explanation is getting old fast, so we argue a lot. I spend most nights alone in bed tossing and turning. How could someone's personality change so drastically in such a short period of time?

Maybe I don't really know who he is? This man with a five-year-old daughter who never visits or is spoken about. Where does this man go night after night?

I am so tired of feeling helpless and alone in this world. I want things to go back to the way they used to be. When we spent our free time together. When I mattered. When I felt loved.

I think of Mama. The long wooden table in the kitchen with the curry stains and knife marks. The red veranda. Lion and Jane Grip. I wish I could call Mama, but she doesn't have a phone. Instead, I write her a letter.

August 1984

Dear Mama,

How are you? I miss you so much. I really didn't want to tell you this, but I don't live with Mommy anymore, but maybe she already told you. I left a year ago and got married to a young man from church. His name is Michael. We live in a place called The Bronx in New York.

Mommy and I don't speak anymore. She tried to stop me from getting married, but I didn't want to live with her anymore and I don't go to her church anymore. I don't want you to think that I was loose, Mama. I didn't have a boyfriend before Michael. I did what you and the pastor said and waited until after I got married. I have never even kissed anybody else. I was really happy at first, because I really love him, and he loves me. I wanted us to have a love like you and Dada.

But now he isn't coming home, and I don't know where he goes. I wish I could see you, Mama, but I don't have any money for a plane ticket. I am still in college and will have my degree soon. Please pray for me. I hope that the arthritis in your knee is getting better. I will send you some money when I can. I hope to hear from you soon.

Your granddaughter,
Donna

Michael gets fired, and my meager salary is not enough to keep us afloat, and we are about to get evicted. It is either a shelter or live with his father in the fifth-floor walkup where I watched a cockroach dying on our wedding day.

I stand at the living room window and stare mindlessly at the cars that move along Bronx Park South. The only good thing about living in my father-in-law's decrepit South

Bronx three-bedroom walk-up apartment is its proximity to the Bronx Zoo and the glimpses of the animals meandering along the grounds. That is what I am hoping for as I gaze through the trees this warm Saturday morning in June, feeling somewhat lost. It has been three months since we made several trips up five flights, dragging labeled boxes and large garbage bags of clothes.

I gaze at my new surroundings. The stained and dingy brown carpeting that lines the hallway, the smell of mildew that hangs in the stale air, the peeling paint, random rodent and water bug sightings. Our bedroom walls are covered with cracks and holes. I decorate it as well as I can. Pictures over things that need to be hidden, a lace doily across the scratched-up dresser and throw pillows on the bed. Michael continues to be scarce, and I remain hopeful that God will save our marriage.

"Good morning." My father-in-law exits his bedroom and walks down the hallway toward the bathroom.

"Good morning, Joe." I smile at my father-in-law. The wild fringe of gray hair around his balding scalp looks almost comical to me.

Joe rarely speaks or leaves his bedroom. He stays in bed and watches television all day, emerging only to go to the bathroom or eat. I feel painfully out of place.

"I can't stand living in this apartment." I complain to Michael one evening.

"I've been filling out a lot of job applications. As soon as I find a job and save up, we will be out of here." His face is serious.

"We need our own place!" I murmur.

"I am doing my best, Donna. Don't unpack everything. I promise you that we won't be here long, babe."

It's a little past 2 a.m. a week later and I need to pee. I wish I didn't have to walk to the bathroom. Rodents roam more freely at nights, despite all the rat traps that my father-in-law has placed strategically around the apartment. I reach for Michael to ask him to walk with me. He is not there. Maybe he is in the bathroom.

I hurry along the dark hallway with a stiff knot tightening in my stomach. Michael is not in the bathroom. Sadness and anger fill me as I hover over the toilet too scared to sit or turn on the lights. The sound causes the hair to rise up on the back of my neck. It is a cross between a chirping and a hissing or maybe hundreds of fingernails tapping against each other. *Tap. Hiss. Tap. Chirp. Tap.* Here in the shadowy gloom of the bathroom, terror mingles with curiosity. I flick the switch and light floods the bathroom. A glistening carpet of light and dark brown cockroaches blankets the wall. I gasp and freeze, my eyes bulging as they crawl jerkily above the tub. Some are on top of each other. Some are trying to fly. Some fall in the tub. I start to itch. My back, my neck, my legs. What if there are others? My eyes quickly flick back and forth scanning the ceiling then the floor and back to the ceiling. My forehead is covered in sweat, and I think that I am going to vomit. I step back slowly. I want to yell but I can't. My throat burns trying to dislodge my silent scream. I keep trying until it finally escapes.

"Joe! Joe!" I shriek.

I get to my father-in-law's bedroom just as he is getting out of bed. Sleepy and confused by my yelling.

"What's wrong?" he asks, studying my face and pushing his feet in his worn-out slippers.

"The bathroom is full of cockroaches. They are everywhere!" I am hyperventilating.

"Okay, okay. Let me see." He hurries past me and I follow at a safe distance behind him. I watch in abject horror from the doorway, but Joe does not appear even remotely concerned as he turns on the hot water, filling up the tub. Thick steam fills the bathroom. I feel faint. He grabs the broom from the corner and begins to sweep them into the tub. Some fall into the scalding water. Some take flight briefly above the tub.

Could this be a nightmare? This is not the fairy tale life I dreamt of living in America or the marriage I wanted with the love of my life. My brain is scrambling trying to process the scene. I can't. I fling the front door open and stagger down the stairs, the sound of my footsteps echoing in the early morning air. Terror, sadness, and complete despair are stifling me. My legs are weak by the time I get outside. I sink to my knees on the sidewalk, bathed in the streetlight on the corner. I cry in the stillness, my chin trembling as if I am a small child. This neighborhood is dangerous, but I don't care what happens to me.

"I can't take this anymore," I whisper to myself. My mind is numb, my thoughts jumbled. I sit on the ground for a while before leaning against the side of the building. I stay in that position on a dangerous corner in the South Bronx until the darkness begins to surrender to daylight. I feel trapped and there is nowhere for me to go. I lost my family when I left the church.

I see him in the distance. Shoulders back, with his soldier-like walk as if he is superior to the world. My tired eyes study him as he gets closer. *You said you love me, dear husband, and I believed you.*

It would have been kinder to just leave me with my mother instead of torturing me.

"What are you doing out here?" Michael looks utterly confused.

My mind is shredded. My body is exhausted. "What am I doing out here? Where the hell were you?" Silence.

"There is an infestation of bugs in your father's apartment, and I want a divorce." I turn and enter the building.

Michael is saying something. I am not listening. I just know that I have to leave. If only I had money or someplace to go.

Now I am doing my best to relax as I wait for my OB/ GYN to give me the results of the blood test. There is that feeling in my belly again. A mixture of nausea and pain that have become my companion for the past two weeks. Plus, I am late. All the reasons why I shouldn't have a child are running rampant in my mind. I have only one semester left before getting my bachelor's degree in Mass Communications and Theatre. That disgusting apartment is not fit for anyone to live in, let alone a newborn baby. I don't think my husband loves me anymore.

The doctor enters the room and settles behind her desk. "You're pregnant." Her words invade my psyche.

"I am?" I try to sound happy.

"Yes, you are. Two months. But I do not recommend that you go through with the pregnancy." I study her face as she turns the pages of the report.

"Why not?" I am confused. For a split second I believe that she knows that my marriage is failing.

"Well, you have several oversized fibroid tumors that should be removed before you have a child. If you go through with it, you are risking your life and that of your child."

"I am a Christian. I don't believe in abortion."

"Well, if you decide to go through with it against my recommendation, you will need to sign this release confirming that I made you aware of the risk." She pushes a document across the desk.

"Thank you. I understand." I sign it and push it back.

"If you go through with this, I am going to recommend strict bed rest for the next seven months and you will also need to see me monthly." She hands me a prescription for prenatal vitamins, and I exit Bronx Lebanon Hospital.

* * *

"We can work it out, Donna." Michael stands over me as I pack a bag.

"I would like that very much. But this is a very high-risk pregnancy and I can't stay in this nasty apartment by myself night after night waiting for you to come home from wherever you go at night." I zip my suitcase.

"So, how long are you going to stay at Ann's mother's house?" Michael looks worried.

"Until this house doesn't make me want to vomit or until you start acting like a husband, whichever comes first."

I spend the next five months in my friend Ann's mother's tiny guest room, most of the time in severe pain. Michael visits once or twice weekly bearing a hefty supply of oranges, to satisfy my only pregnancy craving. I watch soap operas with Ann's grandmother, learn how to crochet and rest as much as I can.

Ann enters my bedroom one evening and sits on the side of the bed. I study my best friend's round belly with a smile. She is also very pregnant, and our babies are due two weeks apart. She looks worried.

"What's wrong? Are you okay?" I struggle to a sitting position.

"My mother and grandmother want you to go back home to the Bronx," she whispers while staring at the floor. My heart drops. I don't want to go back to Michael's father's disgusting apartment.

"Why? Did I do something wrong?"

"No, no," she assures me. "I don't even think that it's you. But when Michael is here, they can't walk around freely in their nightgowns. They want some privacy. I am sorry, Donna."

"Don't be sorry. I understand. I am so grateful to your family for taking me in. Again!" We both laugh, but the thought of returning to that South Bronx apartment fills me with dread and a heavy sadness.

I return to Michael's father's apartment, which is somewhat cleaner and neater. But still no place for our daughter, who arrives a month later at 1:15 a.m. on January 18, 1986. For the next seven months, I let us pretend we are happy new parents, navigating a whirlwind of fatigue, diaper rashes and ear infections. Michael finds a new job as a customer service manager and comes home every evening to play the role of doting husband and father. But it doesn't take long for the novelty of parenthood to wear off for my husband. He abruptly stops coming home after work and disappears until the wee hours of the mornings. He takes out the trash at 6 p.m. one summer evening and returns the next day at 7 a.m.

He walks into our bedroom with a nonchalant "Good morning," bends over our daughter's crib to kiss her before plopping down on the bed. He doesn't look at me or explain his whereabouts. Anger churns and shoots out of me like steaming lava.

"Where were you, Michael?"

He smirks.

"Where were you?" I demand, growing more and more exasperated. "How could you be so inconsiderate? I haven't slept a wink last night thinking that something happened to you."

"Would you please calm down? I am tired." He sits on the bed and kicks off his shoes.

"Tired of what? Where were you?" I shriek.

He ignores me and crawls under the covers and pulls them over his head. "You're annoying me!" he grumbles.

My rage rises and something takes over. I rip the comforter from him and fling it across the room before brushing all his cologne bottles from his side of the dresser with one sweep.

Glass shatters against the wall and a mixture of fragrances wafts through the air. Our daughter's cry fills the room as Michael watches me with a shocked smirk. I place a pacifier in her mouth. She sniffles and settles down. I wipe angry tears and survey our bedroom, feeling sorry for myself.

He is supposed to take care of us. That's what the Bible says.

Without saying a word, Michael jumps up from the bed, grabs his large duffle bag from the closet and proceeds to toss his clothes in. My stomach tilts.

"What are you doing? Where are you going?" Panic fills my belly.

"I am confused about our marriage," he responds without looking at me.

"What are you confused about? We have a child!" I shout at him, pointing at our daughter who is now asleep. He continues to frantically dump his clothes in the duffle bag.

"Please don't go, Michael. Just talk to me," I beg as I carefully pick up shards of glass from the broken cologne bottles and place them in the garbage pail. He continues to pack.

"Are you just going to leave us? How can you just leave us, Michael?" I can't catch my breath. He tosses a twenty-dollar bill on the dresser.

"Michael, I am scared of this apartment!" I step closer to him, pleading. "Please don't leave us here, Michael. I am so scared of the rats and roaches. They are everywhere! What if they bite her? Please don't go, baby. Please stay with us."

"My father is here, Donna. Stop being so damn dramatic!" He glares at me before continuing. "As I said. I am confused about this marriage and I need some time alone. I am going to stay with Carlton. I just need to figure some things out."

He grabs his white down coat and reaches for the doorknob. I block his path with feigned defiance.

"You need time alone? Really? What about me? You are never around to help me with our daughter. What the hell do you mean you need time alone?"

He pushes past me. The tears flow as he slams the door behind him. I sit on the edge of the bed and stare at nothing in particular.

Three weeks pass. No call. No visit. Behind my smile is a desperate woman who is suffering from depression who doesn't want to do this alone. Secretly, I hope that the "absence makes the heart grow fonder" adage will prove true and my husband will come home. It doesn't. Yet somehow I still love him and have loved him from the day we hugged at the back of the theatre.

I am between paychecks at my job as a receptionist at a personnel agency and I need money for Pampers and formula. I dial Michael's friend Carlton's number. My heart races as the phone rings on the other end.

"Hello?" Carlton answers sleepily.

"Hey, Carlton. This is Donna. I am sorry, did I wake you?"

"It's okay. Hey, Donna, whassup?"

"Is Michael there?"

Long silence. I hear him breathing.

"Hello? Are you there? Carlton?" The silence hangs heavily between the lines.

"Yeah. I'm listening. But—why would Michael be here?" He sounds confused.

"He told me that he has been staying with you for the past three weeks. Has he been there?" I know the answer before he responds.

"Donna. I haven't seen Michael in months." More silence. "Look, this is none of my business, but I heard that he is living in Throgs Neck."

My face flushes with embarrassment. "Sorry to bother you, Carlton. Goodnight." I am numb.

Two days later, Michael saunters into the apartment late on a Saturday evening. "Hi," he says dryly, and kisses me on the cheek. "How is my baby girl?" He asks Ava, who is clutching the side of her crib and bouncing with excitement at the sight of her father. He picks her up and tickles her. She gives him a big gummy smile and plays with his necklace.

"So, when are you coming home?" I force a smile. "Are you going to live with Carlton forever?"

"I am staying with him because I just need to clear my head," he answers, while making funny faces at Ava. She giggles.

"You're lying!" I shriek. "I called him on Thursday night, and he told me that he hasn't seen you in months!" I am shaking.

His shock is obvious. "Fine, I am not staying with him, but I am not going to stay here either," he shoots back.

"Why not? I am your wife. This is your child. You moved us into your father's critter-infested apartment and abandoned us. That's not the Bible's version of a good husband," I snap.

"You want to know the truth, Donna?" There is an awkward pause.

"I am leaving you because you gained weight! I am living with and in love with someone else."

I stare at him, unable to process his words or formulate a response. It was as if someone slammed my gut with a sledgehammer. Tears well and roll down my face. He hands me a wad of cash and takes Ava next door to his father's room. I close the door behind them and curl up into a ball on the bed.

Yes. Of course, I gained weight. I had to stay in bed for seven grueling months as our baby competed for space in my fibroid-riddled womb. I hear muffled voices and laughing next door in his father's room, which annoys me. What's there to fucking laugh about?

I wipe my face and walk over to the dirty green paisley couch in the living room, directly across from them. Michael turns to look at me. Our eyes meet briefly. He turns back and continues his conversation with his father. Michael balances Ava on his hip as she rests her head on his shoulder. Michael is grinning and pointing to a stack of pictures in his father's hands. His father moves each one from the top of the pile to the bottom as they snicker. Ava notices me and reaches her arms for me and I go to her. Neither father nor son makes any effort to hide the pictures of my husband's scantily clad nineteen-year-old mistress. Instead, they ogle and lavish each one with laudatory comments about her beauty and perfect body. He knows what he is doing, and he is doing it deliberately.

I have never felt so low, so invisible, so inconsequential. I study my husband's face, his eyes bright with pride about his beautiful young girlfriend. I don't recognize this stranger. This is not the man who hugged me backstage on closing night four years earlier. This is not the man who bought me twenty-three Avon gifts on our first Christmas together. This is not the man with whom I shared wedding vows on a rainy spring morning. His blatant disrespect and cruelty stun me. I gaze down at his father, who sits on the edge of bed, his fat belly jiggling as he throws his head back in no-teeth openmouthed laughter.

I take Ava from Michael's arms. He releases her without even looking at me. I close the bedroom door behind us, turn out the lights, climb under the covers and settle into the warmth and darkness.

At 12:13 a.m., I awaken disoriented and frightened. I hold my breath and listen to the rustling sound. I grab the flashlight that I keep under my pillow and press the "on" bottom. The brightness floods the room as I creep toward my daughter's crib. I point the light around the room, creating different shadows. I hear the sound again. It is definitely coming from the crib. I move faster and point the light along the swaddled body of my daughter.

My entire body stiffens at the sight of something furry slithering across her sleeping face; its long tail meanders along the side of the crib and disappears behind the yellow-and-white crib bumper. I stifle a scream as the hairs at the nape of my neck bristle. I squeeze my eyes tightly and take a deep breath and ever so slowly and deliberately, lift my sleeping baby girl to my chest. She snuggles against me as I crawl onto the bed. With my heartbeat jackhammering in my ears, I tuck the comforter tightly around us. Tears fall here in the dark as rats circle the bed. Terror crawls down my spine. I press the button on the flashlight. The clunk under my thumb is a little comforting as the beam illuminates our huddled frames. I shake the flashlight frantically, hoping the erratic flashes of light will scare them away. They don't. I hold my daughter against me, praying and crying until the first sign of daylight.

I bolt out of bed with a wild and frenzied plan.

I must leave now. Like right this minute.

I make several trips up and down the five flights of stairs with everything that could fit into my dirty brown 10-year-old Chevy Chevette, which is parked in an empty lot across from the building. Sweat causes my shirt to cling to my back and my hair is like a second layer of skin across my face. I am trying to catch my breath as I place Ava in the back seat and buckle her in. I climb into the driver's seat and make sure that the metal slab is completely covering the gaping hole on the floor of the driver's side. I check my rearview mirror; Ava sucks her thumb and peers out the window curiously. She looks so small surrounded by the huge piles of our stuff that are almost obstructing the rear window. My brain is foggy from exhaustion and adrenaline. I hurl questions at myself.

Where are you going? The car is not working.

Have you forgotten that you are terrified of driving? What are you doing?

I ignore the voices in my head and turn the key in the ignition. The car sputters. *Turn. Sputter. Turn. Sputter. Tears. Sobs. Turn.* The car roars to life. I wipe my face with a shaking hand and turn into traffic toward Southern Boulevard. I get to the stop light. I close my eyes and try to calm my breathing. Ava smiles at me in the rearview mirror.

Mommy's gonna get us out of here, baby.

I grip the steering wheel and get ready for the light to change when I see his white down jacket. Michael is waiting in the crosswalk on the other side of Southern Boulevard. He sees me and hurries against the light toward me. *Shit.* What is he doing here?

My insides scream. I just want to go. I just want to go as far away as possible from him and his father and that apartment where rats and betrayal roam freely. The light changes. I press the brakes. The car dies. *Shit. Shit. Shit.* I pump the brakes frantically. *Please start.* He is only yards away. *Please God. Please help me. Please.*

He's at the hood, stomping angrily toward the driver's side. "Daddy!" Ava squeals behind me.

"Yes, baby. It's Daddy." I am stomping on the brakes now. He's at my side mirror when the car roars to life. *Thank you, Jesus!*

I make a quick and jerky right turn onto Southern Boulevard and watch the rearview mirror until I can no longer see the white down jacket. Deep, slow breaths. I turn into the first mechanic shop I see. A middle-aged man with gray hair peeking out from under a baseball cap approaches my car.

"Good morning, Miss," he says cheerily with a thick Spanish accent.

"Good morning, Sir," I respond trying to be as cheerful as possible.

"How can I help you?" he asks, peering into the car at my toddler sleeping against a mound of stuff. I tell him that my car is not working, I am trying to get away from my husband, but I have no money to get it fixed. His smile disappears as he studies me. I try to steady my breathing, expecting him to politely ask me to leave the premises. I have no plan B.

"Pull it over to the side." He points to a corner of the mechanic shop where men in oil-stained blue overalls are busy tinkering under hoods.

"Let me take a look. I will fix it if I can, and I won't charge you." His kindness stuns me. I think of Mama's words: God has his hand on your life and no matter what happens leave it to him. He'll fix it.

This angel opens my door and I step out and open the back door and take Ava into my arms. I feel him watching me as I wipe hot tears with the back of my hands.

"Have a seat in the waiting area. It is warm in there. Have some tea. I need about an hour." He smiles and wipes his hands with a yellow rag as he walks away.

I wait with the other customers. My mind races as Ava nestles in my lap, thumb in her mouth and head against my chest. Two hours pass before the mechanic sticks his head in and beckons for me to follow him. I zip up Ava's snowsuit and pull her hat over her ears, before taking her hand and stepping out into the cold January air. We walk hurriedly toward the mechanic, who is smiling at us. Smiling is good.

"I did the best that I could. It's not perfect, but I think that it should get you to where you are trying to go," he says proudly and pinches Ava's cheek. She smiles at him.

"Thank you so much, Sir. May God bless you."

"Good luck, Miss." He turns and heads to the other side of the lot. I open the passenger door, Ava climbs in and I buckle her seatbelt.

When I stand back up, I feel him next to me, before I see him. His white down jacket is beside me. I try to move but Michael blocks my path.

"I knew you wouldn't get far with this piece of shit." He smirks.

"Get out of my way Michael," I hiss.

"Where are you going with my car?"

"Your car? I paid the $350 dollars for this car. It is my piece of shit. May I remind you that it is registered in my name. I pay the insurance and the tickets that you racked up without telling me. So, explain how this is your car?" I am shaking.

"Well, I am the one who paid to get it fixed when it broke down," he shoots back.

"Of course, you did. You needed to drive your whore around!" I yell back.

"Whatever, Donna! I paid money for that license plate holder." He points to the shiny Jamaican flag holder which looks ridiculous on an old dilapidated car, which has a gaping hole through which one can see the road as we drive.

"You're an idiot." My spunk surprises even me.

He slams me against the car and grabs the shoulder straps of my purse. "Where the fuck are you going?" he barks in my face.

"You live with someone else. Why do you care?" His eyes are daggers. People are beginning to stare, and even my mechanic angel is glaring at him.

Ava is crying. I force a conciliatory smile, trying to calm him.

"Look babe, I am going to visit Ann, just for the weekend. I will be back tomorrow, and we'll talk," I lie. I am still pinned against the car. "Michael, please let go of my bag. People are staring," I plead and look into eyes that used to love me.

"Fuck them," he growls.

There is a long awkward pause before he releases my bag. I jump in the car and lock the doors. I heave with sobs as I watch my husband walk off the lot and hurry around the corner. I take a deep breath and turn the key in the ignition with trembling hands and cautious optimism. I am relieved as the engine hums. I check the rearview mirror and wave at my angel before cautiously merging into traffic with great unease and agonizing slowness. Car horns blare and startle me. I clutch the steering wheel and head nowhere in particular.

I cruise through Harlem, unsure of how I got there. Then the West Side Highway. I make it to the BQE, praying that this is a nightmare. I am lost in neighborhoods with fruit names. I keep going; a sense of desperation causes my body to tremble. Soon I will wake up in Michael's arms and tell him about a frightful dream.

I listen to the hum of the engine. Dusk is falling. Something catches my eye in the rearview mirror. A thick cloud of exhaust fumes fills the air and a green trail of anti-freeze snakes along the highway. It takes a few seconds for it to register that it is coming from my car. I turn off at the next exit and pull onto the side of the road just before the car jerks violently and dies.

The events of the past few weeks have now beaten me into submission. There is nothing left in my emotional tank. I remove Ava, my purse and her baby bag from the car and I take her hand. We walk toward a small park where I place Ava on a bench, wrap a blanket around her and give her the last cheese sandwich. I sit next to her and look off into the distance.

"Do you want us to push the car onto the side street for you?" I jump at the sound and sight of four young men looking down at me.

"If you want to." I shrug nonchalantly. "But I don't have any money to pay you."

I expect them to keep moving. They don't. I place Ava on my lap and hold her close. They hurry over to the car. One climbs into the driver's seat and the other three circle the car, pushing and shoving and pushing and shoving until it is sitting on the side street across from me. They walk toward us.

"I can only afford to give you $5." I show them the $50 bill that has been balled up in my fist. The oldest-looking one takes it and they make change among themselves. He hands me two twenty-dollar bills and five singles with an awkward smile and a "Good luck lady" before they all head down the block.

I sigh with relief and deposit a quarter in a payphone and dial Ann's number. I ask her to ask her mom if we could stay with them until I find a place. Her mom agrees.

Tears of relief crawl down my face as we settle in the back of a cab. I stare into the darkness and chuckle at the coincidence. Ann's mother's home became my haven when I ran away from my mother's apartment to marry Michael, and when I needed a less scary place to stay during my pregnancy. It's about to play the same role as I run again. This time, as I run away from Michael.

I find a basement apartment within two weeks in the Cypress Hills section of Brooklyn. Michael visits his daughter a few times, before he disappears from our lives completely, but not before confessing a few sins.

He has never been faithful. Three different women spent the night in my bed during my three-night hospital stay after giving birth to our child. The night he called me in a panic and told me that he had been mugged of his cash, wedding band and credit card, was a ruse. There was no mugging. He concocted the story to conceal the loss of his wedding band during a late-night tryst with a prostitute. The woman who was sitting on our bed the evening I arrived home unexpectedly with Chinese food, was not a co-worker dropping off documents as he had claimed. She was his mistress. My timing was apparently perfect.

I write another letter to Mama:

February 1988

Dear Mama,

How are you? I hope that the high blood pressure and the pain in your knee is not giving you too much trouble. I am trying to come up with the money to come to see you. My husband left me and the baby and moved in with another woman. He doesn't give me any money for the baby, so things are very hard. I hope that you will be able to meet your great-granddaughter one of these days. Her name is Ava and she is a very good baby. Please pray for us, Mama, because things are very hard right now. I will pray for you as well. I hope to see you soon.

Your loving granddaughter,
Donna

Fourteen

A YEAR IN THE LIFE

2017

JAVIER AND I ARE SITTING IN TAO, a Pan-Asian restaurant in midtown Manhattan. TAO is known for its club-like vibe, dimly lit setting, Asian motifs and a towering 16-foot-tall Buddha that hovers above a large reflecting pool. The restaurant is full, and the noise level is high. I look around at the busy tables and see businessmen sharing wine, women collapsing with giggles, and couples holding hands across candle-lit tables.

By candlelight, Javier's brown eyes glisten and glow with a mischievous glint. I stare at him adoringly. He notices me watching him and a grin flashes across his face. He reaches for my hand.

"Happy one year anniversary, *chica*. Thanks for the best year of my life. I love you."

"Happy anniversary, Javier. I love you, too." I beam. "Let's check out this menu, the waiter will be back soon."

We settle on two signature dishes: the Chilean sea bass for me and the Kung Pao chicken for him. My mind careens back to the night in my living room a year ago, when he confessed to being an ex-con. How I crumbled on the couch after he left, disappointed, and confused. How I have spent the past year remodeling him like an old house. Writing his resume and cover letters, doing mock interviews with him, connecting him with my business owner friends in my network who agreed to do me the favor of conducting exploratory interviews with someone who just needs a break.

A year later, here we sit. He works nights in a factory, and he has a few interviews lined up for mailroom, cable technician and call-center jobs. I have met some members of his family, and he, mine. We are planning a spring cruise for my birthday in May and my initials are etched in large dark letters across his chest. He has become my soft place to fall, and I, his.

"You didn't think that we would make it this far, did you, my love?" His voice pulls me back.

"If I am being completely honest, no," I reply with a grin.

He blows me a kiss and I pretend to catch it. Our waiter returns with our meals.

"How is the apartment search going?" Javier asks as he breaks a piece of bread and dips it into the sauce from his chicken dish.

"That is rather random. Don't you think?" I stare up at him curiously.

"Just wondering. You have been looking through real estate listings for months now. Just curious, that's all," he replies casually.

I had seriously started looking to buy an apartment in Manhattan about a year before meeting Javier. Although I love my beautiful apartment in the high-rise building on the Upper East Side, complete with the amenities of a four-star hotel, it does not belong to me. Plus, I would probably pay the same amount, or less, in mortgage payments as I do in rent, and would become a homeowner again. Eight years earlier, I had sold my home in Brooklyn and moved into the city. I am again drawn to the pride of home ownership, the sense of accomplishment and the financial investment it offers as I approach retirement. I have spent countless hours perusing real estate property listings and studying walkthrough videos on different websites.

Some had the square footage of glorified walk-in closets, were "walk-ups" and others, well, I simply couldn't afford. I was still waiting for "the one."

"Still looking," I reply. "Real estate in Manhattan is not for the faint of heart."

"Well, with the amount of money that you would spend buying a co-op or condo in Manhattan, you could buy my cousin's house five times and still have money left over," he states confidently.

"Do we have to talk about your cousin's house now? This is supposed to be a celebration. It is our anniversary," I protest.

"I will say one last thing and I will leave it alone. Okay?" He raises his eyebrows as if seeking permission to continue. I nod reluctantly and roll my eyes.

"You are planning to retire in six years. Right?" he asks.

"Yes. So?" I study his face, not sure where the conversation is going.

"Don't forget that my cousin's house is a three-family home with a brand-new roof. The framing is already done. It's a steal for the price and it's just sitting there. By the time you retire, it would have paid for itself with the rental income. You will never have to pay rent or a mortgage again for the rest of your life."

"I do not want to talk about this now. Okay?"

"I know, *chica*. I would just hate to see you lose out on a great deal."

"I thought that you were going to say one thing," I say, using my index and middle fingers to create air quotes to accentuate the word *one*. We both laugh.

"I know. But the house has been sitting there for eight years now, and—"

"We already had this conversation, Javier!" I interrupt him. "I have no desire to be a landlord. I just want to buy a small place on the Upper East Side and enjoy a retirement free from tenant drama," I remind him.

"But you wouldn't have to do anything," he persists. "I would live in the basement and take care of the tenants until you retire. I would be the super and we could live there together when you retire." He is unrelenting.

I put my fork down and glare at him.

"Okay, I will change the subject," he says dejectedly. "When is your bunion surgery?"

"Your mind is all over the place tonight, isn't it?"

He shrugs indifferently.

"My bunion surgery isn't scheduled yet, but it will probably be in late May. Once I have the actual date, I will let you know, because I will need you to take me home and take care of me," I remind him.

"Of course I am going to take you home and take care of you! Who else is gonna wait on you hand and foot, silly?" He looks up from the dessert menu with a smirk. "Saw what I did there? Hand and foot?" We both laugh and soon we are armed with two spoons and digging into a serving of banana pudding.

"Will you at least look at the house for shits and giggles? It's a nice drive to Waterbury, Connecticut. Something to do one of these weekends and—"

I frown at him mid-bite.

He cringes and waits for a verbal attack. "No pressure. I just really want you to see it." He looks at me with a pout.

"Fine. I will look at it. Could you please shut up now about this stupid house?" I grumble.

He blows me a kiss and I pretend to catch it.

Fifteen

SEE NO EVIL

KENNY G'S "FOREVER IN LOVE" fills the Queens, New York, makeshift banquet hall chapel as my bridal party sashays down the aisle in synchronized movement. I stand behind the red velvet curtain and try to slow my heartbeat with deep breaths as I prepare to marry Jack.

I look over at my father and study the gentleness of his smile and feel happy that he is here to walk me down the aisle. Although he and my mother never married, I have always yearned for a relationship with him and cherish the faint childhood memory of the day we met on the red veranda and the day he took my sister and me to Coney Island. When I moved to America, we saw each other from time to time, but really connected at a time when I was filled with profound sadness after my marriage to Michael imploded nine years earlier—a time when he bought me a bed and filled my fridge with groceries.

My father, a man I am getting better acquainted with, paces from side to side. Through a slit in the curtain, I watch the flower girl scatter white rose petals along the satin runner. Soon, contemporary jazz is replaced by the muffled shuffling of chairs across the wooden floor, as everyone stands. The bridal chorus swells and all heads turn to the back of the room in anticipation of my entrance. I place my hand in the crook of Daddy's elbow as the curtain rises.

The rustling sound of my tulle wedding dress against the satin runner fills the room. The photographer walks backward in front of me, his large black camera flashing steadily. Through my veil, I study the grainy images of the fourteen people in my bridal party, standing on either side of the wedding arch at the front of the room. The chairs on the aisle are bursting with white balloons and wine-colored streamers flutter behind them. I squeeze my sweaty palms against my bouquet as I gaze at my husband-to-be.

Jack looks regal in a black single-breasted tuxedo with a white wing-collared shirt. We get to the end of the aisle and my father hugs me and passes me on to him. Everything is a blur.

Vows.

Rings.

Prayer.

I focus on Uncle Errol's voice. The same voice that used to bring me such joy during my two summer vacations in Brooklyn, New York when he lived right next door with his wife. When we all laughed at his goofy shenanigans and danced to reggae beats in the middle of my mother's living room. My uncle, the friend of Bob Marley, is now dressed in a black velour clergy robe with gold etchings on the sleeve. A black satin stole with gold crosses drapes around his neck, with the two ends hanging parallel to each other down the front of his body.

"By the power vested in me by the State of New York, I now pronounce you husband and wife. You may now kiss your bride."

Jack lifts my veil and kisses me as everyone cheers. We hold each other's gaze before linking arms and walking up the aisle with the attendants in tow. Secretly, I am hoping that the marriage fixes him. Us. But for now, I smile brightly. Because that is what you are supposed to do on your wedding day.

* * *

I had met Jack seven years earlier.

It's May of 1989, seven days after my twenty-seventh birthday and almost two years after I drove away from Michael in a broken-down Chevy Chevette with a one-year-old in the back seat. It is a crisp morning as I walk hand in hand with my three-year-old to the babysitter. Jack stands at the side of her house scribbling notes on a clipboard as I help my toddler up the stairs.

"Good morning." He smiles with a touch of shyness. He is tall and lanky with an average-looking face. His Con Edison cap is twisted off to the side.

"Hi," I reply as I ring the doorbell to the babysitter's house. She opens it and my daughter pushes past her to join the other children that are already playing on the floor. I hurry down the stairs, feeling his eyes on me.

"I didn't get your name."

"I didn't give it," I reply with indifference.

"Well, I'm Jack. Jack Hayes." He extends his hand for a handshake.

"I am late. Must catch my train." I give him a quick shake and continue walking.

He hurries alongside me. "I don't want you to miss your train, but are you married?" He pries.

"Divorced."

"You are very beautiful. I would love to take you to dinner."

"I don't think so." I turn my head slightly to study him.

His face is long and angular with full brown eyes and deep creases in his forehead.

"Here's my number in case you change your mind," he says, ripping a corner of paper from the clipboard and scribbling a phone number and handing it to me. "This is my home number, call anytime. If I am not home, just leave a message with my aunt."

I take it from him and hurry up the stairs to the train station.

"Call me!" He shouts from the bottom of the stairs.

I am scared to get close to another man after Michael. I toy with the idea of throwing it in the trash but tuck it in my purse instead, before boarding the 8:05 J train to my receptionist job in midtown Manhattan.

Two weeks later, on a warm Saturday morning, I wake with a heavy sadness crawling over me. I look around my small windowless basement apartment, my three-year-old's sleeping frame and the food that my best friend Ann's grandmother dropped off the evening before. I gaze at the cans of pork and beans, Chef Boyardee, fruit cocktail, a bag of potatoes, a loaf of Wonder Bread, cheese slices and Corn Flakes that line my counter. Michael refuses to pay child support. We have no extra money. No food. I feel like a sad and pathetic charity case. The depression has been heavy. Growing. I need a change of scenery. I fish the little piece of paper out of my purse and dial Jack's number.

Let's see what this one is all about. "Hello?" Her voice is young.

"Hi. May I please speak with Jack?"

"Sure. May I say who is calling?"

"This is Donna."

"Jack! Phone! It's Donna!" she shouts.

I wait for Jack to get on the line.

"Hey, Donna. Glad to hear from you." He sounds bubbly.

"Hi Jack. How are you?"

We make awkward small talk before he gets to the point. "Would you like to go to see *Hear No Evil, See No Evil* with me next weekend?"

"Sure, why not?" I hear myself say. I had been wanting to see the Richard Pryor and Gene Wilder movie ever since it came out. We spend the next Saturday before Memorial Day together. The movie and then brunch. We sit in a diner for two hours, making pleasant conversation over breakfast food and getting acquainted. He was born in Brooklyn but raised by his grandmother in Wilmington, North Carolina. Played high school basketball against Michael Jordan's team. Has never been married and has no children. He will be moving out of his aunt's apartment soon. He reaches across the table for my hand, but I don't feel the pull to touch him or be touched by him. I give him my hand and he puts it to his lips and kisses it.

He brings me home from our third date. We are sitting on the porch of my landlord's house and the guilt sits in my chest. I gaze at the sunset. The sky is all aglow with bursts of yellow and orange. I take a deep breath.

"Jack, I have something to tell you."

"Is everything okay?"

"Everything is fine." My hands shake. I pause. "I am still legally married." I watch his eyes darken. I look at the floor and continue. "My husband left us almost two years ago but I can't afford a lawyer right now. I just want you to know the truth."

I can see the anger boiling behind his eyes. He clenches his fists and jumps to his feet before glaring down at me.

"You lied to me? You lied to me?" he hisses through clenched teeth. "Just as I was beginning to have feelings for you, you lay this on me? You are a married woman!" He screams.

"Okay, calm down!" I try to ease the tension. "We have both moved on. I just can't afford to—"

"Save it!" he interrupts, before storming down the steps toward his car.

I watch as he climbs in and speeds away. I lie awake in bed that night feeling confused and mortified by what I consider to be an overreaction. He doesn't call for a few days and I don't call him. We see each other the following weekend and his temperament is softer and he apologizes for his outburst.

"Will you make me a promise?" he asks as we sit on the couch. "Promise me that you will always tell me the truth." He places his arm around my shoulder and looks into my eyes, "And I promise to do the same. No matter what."

"Okay. I promise. Friends?" I ask.

"Friends," he answers with a grin.

As I sit there staring into Jack's brown eyes, I want to feel a romantic spark. I want us to have chemistry. There is none. However, since meeting him, I no longer sit in a windowless basement apartment on the weekends with my three-year-old trying to heal from my disastrous marriage. He takes us to amusement parks, the movies and the mall. I feel myself rebooting, coming back to life. Love isn't everything.

It is a summer afternoon in July, and he is bringing us home after a fun day at Coney Island. He pulls into a parking spot in front of the house. I exit the car and remove Ava from the back seat. Jack opens the trunk of his car and something catches my eye. Toys.

"Whose toys are those?" I ask pointing to a yellow truck, an Alf Doll and large colorful blocks.

"Oh, those?" He slams the trunk and turns to face me. "They belong to my niece and nephew," he explains before changing the subject.

I wonder why his niece or nephew hasn't come up in conversation in almost three months. The toys-in-the-trunk sighting leaves me suspicious. I tell my co-worker Tonya and we hatch a plan. It is very common for *Newsday* telemarketers to call and inquire about the demographics of a household. She decides to impersonate one for fun.

During our lunch hour, Tonya presses the speaker button and dial Jack's telephone number. My heart races. Jack's Aunt with the youthful voice answers.

"Hi, I am calling from *Newsday* and was wondering if you could spare a few minutes." Tonya stifles a giggle. "We are collecting demographic data of households in your Bedford Stuyvesant neighborhood."

"Okay," she responds.

"Thank you." Tonya says, giving me the thumbs up with a wink. "So, what is the make-up of your household?" Her voice fills the conference room.

"There are four people in my household. Me. My five-year-old daughter, Shara. My one- year-old son Ricky. And my husband, Jack."

I feel the blood drain from my face. Tonya hangs up the phone and we both stare at it. My mind gallops back to the evening when I told Jack that I am still married. I can still feel the heat of his belligerence, his look of disappointment. I now know that we are in similar situations, with one colossal difference: His wife and two children are at home waiting for him. A familiar crippling feeling covers me. I have had enough of these feelings to last a lifetime.

That evening Jack picks me up from the train station. Being near him triggers a hot bubbling rage in my stomach. He senses it.

"Why are you so quiet?"

"You lied to me," I whisper.

"What are you talking about?" He pulls over to the side of the road and turns to look at me.

"Are you married?" Silence.

"Well. Are you?"

"I can explain."

"Please do," I interrupt. "Did you forget to tell me that you have a wife and two children?"

"I can explain," he mutters. "We were forced to marry at a young age because she got pregnant."

I stare straight ahead as he continues.

"I sleep on the couch. The marriage is over. I told you that I am looking for my own place. Remember?"

I turn my head slowly and deliberately until our eyes lock. "Yes. I remember. You said you are looking to move out of your aunt's house. But there is no aunt, Jack. No aunt, just a wife!" I screech. The anger feels like heat crawling along my skin.

"I am sorry. I didn't think you would understand."

"Yet when I came clean about my marital status, you made me feel like dirt. Who does that?"

"I am so sorry. I was wrong." He sounds desperate.

"Please take me home, Jack." I turn my head to look out the window. "I just want to go home."

"I am telling you the truth. You can ask my mother if you don't believe me," he pleads.

"Take me home. Please," I repeat. I stare straight ahead as he pulls in front of my apartment. I step out and turn to face him. "I don't think I want to see you anymore."

I lock the apartment door behind me. I don't pick up the phone when he calls thirty-one times.

* * *

"May I introduce to you for the first time, Mr. and Mrs. Jack Hayes!" The DJ's voice echoes through the reception hall above thunderous applause. Jack takes my hand and leads me to the dance floor for our first dance to Michael Jackson's "Lady of My Life." I feel Jack's warm hand at the small of my back as he laces the other in mine. All eyes are on us.

The room buzzes with excited chatter. We hold each other close and move in delicate circles. My wedding dress swirls and flows. I rest my head against his tall frame. We float and twist across the room, smiling as camera lights flash and twinkle. "You look beautiful in your dress."

"Thanks. You clean up real nice yourself." I plaster on a smile. We pose for the photographer before mingling with our guests as man and wife. Two hours into the reception, I feel it: A panic that burns like a knot of fire in my chest. My breaths come in gasps. My eyes scan the room until I find my husband, the source of my anxiety. He is talking to his mom on the other side of the room. He tilts his head back and laughs. I need air.

"If anyone asks, I am in the bathroom," I lean over and whisper to my older sister Grace.

"Want me to come with you and help you with your frilly fancy frock?" She chuckles and shoots a playful glance at me from across the rim of her champagne glass.

"Nah, I'm okay. I will be right back," I respond with a giggle. I hike up my dress and hurry along the corridor toward the bathroom and rush into a stall. My breathing is jagged. I sit on the cool lid of the toilet, trying to steady my breathing. *What the hell did you just do?* The voice in my head screams.

One part of me is hopeful that this marriage will fix us. But another part, the deep-down-inside-the-walls-of-my-soul part of me, knows otherwise. I have been living with Dr. Jekyll and Mr. Hyde for the past seven years. I just married them both.

My mind careens back to that early November morning in 1989, six months after meeting him at the babysitter's house. The shrill and unrelenting sound jerks me awake. Startled and dazed, I sit up in bed and squint at the large red numbers that stare at me in the darkness from my nightstand: 2:15 a.m. The bell rings again. And again. And again. I leap out of bed and grab my robe. I glance at my three-year-old sleeping peacefully in her crib, thumb-in-mouth against the wall of our tiny bedroom. I hurry through the living room and open the door of my basement apartment. I feel the frigid November air creeping around me as I move across the cold concrete toward the main door. I hear a sniffing sound. I rub my eyes and peek through the peephole suspiciously. My breathing hitches.

"Jack, what are you doing here?" I whisper. The sallow porch light illuminates his face. "She threw me out. Can we talk?" His voice sounds muffled on the other side. I lean against the bright green door for what seems like minutes. My brain is tangled.

Go away.

Figure it out.

I don't need another liar.

These are things I really want to say. But it is freezing, and he is crying, and I am me.

I acquiesce and reach up to remove the chain before turning the lock. I pull the door open and shiver from the icy air. Jack enters my apartment slowly and sits on the edge of the couch. I close the door behind us and study him from the doorway. His face and eyes are red. His long legs extend from his six-foot frame and stretch halfway across my tiny living room. He shivers. His tattered brown suitcase is still on this lap. He looks like a lost little boy and I feel pity for him.

"Would you like something hot to drink?"

He shakes his head and stares straight ahead. "I am so embarrassed right now. But I just couldn't take it anymore." His voice shakes.

"What happened?" I ask.

"We fought and she threw my things out into the hallway and threatened to call the cops." He leans back and places his hands over his face. "I didn't want to leave my kids."

"You mean the kids you denied having?" I grumble before taking a seat at the other end of the couch.

"I am really sorry that I did that. I have been beating myself up since that day. I just couldn't figure out how to tell you about my situation. It's not easy for someone to understand. I was so wrong. Please forgive me."

Silence.

"Can I stay with you for a week or two until I find my own place? I promise to stay out of your way."

Tell him no, Donna. Tell. Him. No. You can't save everybody!

I walk into my bedroom, grab a pillow and a blanket from the closet and hand them to him. "Make yourself comfortable on the couch. We'll talk in the morning." I close my bedroom door and climb under the covers, and sink back into my childhood, when I would do anything to feel less alone. I am doing it again and I don't know how to stop.

Two weeks turn into two months. He introduces me to his mother, his sisters and stepfather. His mother is a tall Southern woman with long brown hair and kind eyes. His stepfather is a short and slight man with jerry curls and a sweet Southern charm. They welcome us. One day after a now-recurring Sunday dinner, his mother takes me to her bedroom. We sit on the bed.

"My son is a very good person." She holds my gaze. "He tried really hard to work at his marriage. They just couldn't fake it anymore."

"Mary, why is he so angry all the time?" I ask. She drops her voice to a whisper.

"That man out there." She nods toward the living room, where her husband, Jack, my daughter and his children are playing and watching a movie. "He used to beat the shit out of me." Her voice trails off before continuing. "He used to kick me off the bed and dare me to get up. Jack tried to save me. He would drag his drunk-ass stepfather off me. That's when I noticed a change in him. He was mad all the time. All the time. That is why I sent him to Atlanta to live with my sister." She sighs.

"He scares us," I whisper. I stand and close her bedroom door. "He goes from being super nice to a raging lunatic in a matter of seconds. It's as if he has two personalities."

"He needs to see a psychiatrist to manage his anger issues. I have told him that over and over again." She shakes her head. "But he wouldn't hurt a fly. He loves you and those kids. You are all going to be okay. I am going to keep you all in my prayers."

Earlier that day, Jack had smashed a glass across the wall because he couldn't find his keys.

* * *

A stroke takes Mama on a Saturday morning in January 1990.

My mind rushes back to the summer of 1977, the last time I saw her. I was fifteen years old and had settled into my new life in New York City. The summer before I started my sophomore year in high school, my mother sent me back to Jamaica to spend the summer with Mama.

Although it has only been a year, it feels strange to be back. I push open the large metal gate and walk across the yard. Everything looks smaller. The house. Mama's garden of beautiful vibrant flowers. The ackee tree. The outhouse. I feel like a little girl again as I walk up to the front door across the red veranda, dragging my luggage behind me. Mama comes rushing out the door, her warm face cracks into a wide smile.

"Lawd, let me look pon you!" She turns me around and laughs. "What a way you grow big!"

"Hello, Mama." I embrace her in a tight hug.

"Come in out of the hot sun." I move through the house of my youth and memories rush back. The side of the table where the little black-and-white television set sat. The window that I peeked through before sneaking out to comfort animals that were tied to the death tree. The long wooden table with the knife marks and curry stains that became a staple of my childhood. The pictures of my parents that I prayed to. "Me thank the good Lord me get to see you again before he calls me home. Come eat something." Mama places a full plate of stewed chicken, white rice, green bananas and fried plantains in front of me. I slowly savor a bite with closed eyes. There is nothing like Mama's cooking.

"Mama, how have you been?" I ask and chomp on a piece of fried plantain.

"What you say?" Her hearing is going.

"How have you been?" I repeat louder.

She raises her hand and looks to the ceiling "I am carrying on 'til the good Lord sees fit to call me home."

"Yes, Mama."

"Oonu go to church on Sunday?"

"Yes, Mama. We go a lot." I take a sip of sorrel and smile at her.

"Praise the Lord." She plops down in the chair across from me and reaches for her chipped white enamel mug and slurps fresh mint tea with condensed milk. Mama just turned seventy-one, but she looks twenty years younger. Her dark skin is tight, and her eyes are as bright as ever. She moves about the kitchen as she did when I was a little girl. Except for a little hearing loss and arthritis in her knees, Mama shows no sign of slowing down.

For the next six weeks, I am not fifteen, I am back to being the little girl who holds the container of clothespins while Mama hangs the clothes on the line and carries water from the communal pipe. I grease and comb her gray hair the way she used to comb mine. The one thing I did not miss, however, is the outdoor pit toilet and the horrible smell. I do my business and rush out holding my nose, to Mama's amusement. She tells me who died, who is dying, who is working Obeah and who has had Obeah worked on them.

I tell her about school and church and life in America. We watch television, reminisce and make weekly trips to the market. A heavy sadness fills my belly as I prepare to leave and go back to New York. I look around the house of my childhood. This is a place where pieces of my soul sit in the walls, on the small bed where I slept, in the grass where lizards crept and in the corner of this red veranda. Memories—some fond, some painful—hang heavily in me. I can almost hear our laughter as children played on the veranda, the caring call of Mama telling us that supper is ready, the heaviness of the nights after everyone left suddenly.

Mama hands me a bag of snacks for the plane. I take a mental photograph of the woman who has been more of a mother than a grandmother. "Thanks for coming to see the old lady. It was really good to see you before my eyes close."

"It was really good to see you too, Mama. I am going to miss you."

"Keep up your book learning and remember that you are special to the good Lord. He has his hands on your life and no matter what, trust him always."

"Goodbye, Mama."

"Make sure you write me and come back and see me, if the good Lord say the same." I can see the tears forming.

"Okay, Mama. I am going now. Junior is probably waiting down the road." I give her a hug and choke back the tears.

* * *

After Mama dies, something in me breaks and I feel myself crawling into an invisible shell. The sadness is almost unbearable as the weight of her loss presses against my shoulders. I regret that she didn't get a chance to meet her great-granddaughter before she passed. I can't even afford a plane ticket to go to the funeral. I am filled with gratitude to Mama for taking care of me when my mother left. I know now more than ever how important it is to have someone in your corner, come what may. Mama was my person. Knowing that she is gone fills me with a void I cannot articulate.

Godspeed, Mama.

Jack and I have been living together for six months. It's a typical Wednesday morning and we are all getting ready to start the day. Jack is having a heated conversation with his ex-wife about money. Arguments with her always send him into a tailspin.

"I need twenty dollars," he says as he drives me to the train station after we dropped Ava off at the babysitter.

"I don't have it, Jack. I just paid the rent." My voice is almost a whisper.

"You don't have twenty dollars?" His anger is ripe. He slams his hand against the steering wheel. I wince. I have learned to say little when he is in this state. He pulls up to the train station and I quickly hop out of the car and hurry down the subway stairs. Suddenly he is standing beside me as my nervous hands try to insert the token.

"Okay. How about five dollars?" his voice booms. People stare.

"Jack, I just gave you money yesterday for gas and I just paid the—"

"You don't have five dollars?" He cuts me off. I watch the familiar storm brewing in his eyes. I scan the platform for a police officer. None. He holds my gaze. His face contorts. His jaw clenches. I try to insert the token into the slot, almost paralyzed with fear. He lurches toward me with a wild look in his eyes. I step backward as dread makes the rounds through my body. His foot lands solidly against my hip. I stumble backward as he turns and climbs the subway stairs onto Flatbush Avenue.

A woman rushes over. "Are you okay, ma'am?"

"I'm okay. Thank you." My voice is thick with shame. *No! I'm not okay. I am far from okay.*

"Are you sure, ma'am? Should I try to find a cop?"

I shake my head, and hurry through the turnstile and onto the train. I sit by the window of the subway car and process the searing pain that is vibrating along the right side of my body. I look out the window into the darkness as the train rumbles through the tunnel and welcome familiar tears. Later that night, I call his mother and tell her. She asks me to hand him the phone. He sits with the phone pressed hard against his ear.

His voice drops to a whisper as he stares at the floor. "I know, Ma. I'm sorry, Ma. I know." He hangs up the phone and a deluge of apologies follow.

In the summer of 1990, we move to a bigger apartment, and I have surgery to remove the fibroids that were discovered during my pregnancy five years earlier. Jack springs into care-taker mode. He picks me up from the hospital with a pillow to hold against the incision as he slowly navigates around pot-holes from Manhattan to Brooklyn. He fills my prescriptions. He cooks for me. He cares for Ava. He holds cold rags against my head. He wraps me in his arms until I sleep. The glare is gone from his eyes. Something has changed, and I start to feel pangs of hope and affection for Jack. He proposes.

I am in a cold bathroom stall on my 1996 wedding day. I reapply my smile and make-up before hurrying back to the reception hall.

Within six months after our wedding, one of my neigh-bors gingerly places a domestic abuse hotline card in my hand and inquires if my daughter and I need help getting to a shelter. I reassure her that I am not in any danger. After all, I have been kicked only once. Sure, he holds me down and screams in my face.

But I scream back. Although he is over six feet tall, he is thin. His booming voice makes him scarier than he is. He doesn't mean it. After all, it isn't really abuse if he takes his anger out on dishes, mugs, the doors and the furniture. He loves me. See, lady, there are no bruises, black eyes or police reports. He returned the gun to the precinct as part of the NYPD Gun Buyback Program. The holes in the walls and the cracks in the doors are nicely hidden under pretty wallpaper borders. So, we're okay.

I secretly look at several apartments but change my mind just short of signing each lease. What if he finds us? I am haunted by news stories of murder-suicides. I pack and unpack eight times.

In 1998, two years after our wedding, I have my second surgery. Nice Jack to the rescue once again. My career in the financial services industry is flourishing and soon I am promoted to Vice President. In 2000, I purchase a house without any financial assistance from him. He seems calmer in our new space.

"I am going to get a surprise for you," Jack says as he heads out the door on a warm Saturday morning in August 2001.

"A surprise? What kind of surprise?"

"If I told you, it wouldn't be a surprise now, would it?" Jack grins at me as he backs out of the driveway. I smile knowingly. He always buys mangos for me on Saturday mornings.

Hours later, the doorbell rings, I peer through the blinds. I see the car in the garage, but no sign of him. I open the door slowly to see a black and white bundle of fur roaming my porch. She is unreasonably cute. Her alert pointy ears and striking blue almond-shaped eyes take my breath away.

She walks into the house with a figure-eight-shaped chew toy hanging from her mouth as if she owns the joint.

My sixteen-year-old daughter shrieks with delight. I glance at Jack who is leaning against the car with a wide grin as I follow our furry visitor into the house. I name our eight-week-old Siberian husky puppy Cheyenne. We bond over her adorability and puppy antics. There is a warm feel to our home for the first time in a very long time.

It is short-lived. By the fall of 2001, he is unhinged again. He grabs me from the street and pushes me in the car. He speeds and weaves in and out of traffic to scare me as I cling to the grip handle in the car's ceiling. Screaming. Begging. He smashes my dishes in the sink, causing shards of glass to splatter everywhere. I am too terrified to leave.

I am cooking dinner. The jingle of his keys announces his arrival. My insides tighten.

"Hey Jack," I say, forcing cheerfulness, trying to assess his mood.

"Sometimes I feel like killing myself and everything in this house," he growls and tosses his keys on the dining room table. It crashes against the silver vase with a loud clang. Terror crawls up my body and settles in my throat.

"Jack, don't start or I am going to call the cops." He watches me as I step away from the stove. We lock eyes for what seems like an eternity. I feel the cold chill move up my spine and cover my head. But I hold his stare and push down the sludge of panic.

"Call them. I dare you. Call them!" He rushes toward me, grabs my shoulders and stares into my eyes. "I will leave this house in one of two ways. In handcuffs or a body bag. You pick!" He whispers in my ear.

"I want a divorce, Jack." My voice feels calm and steady even though it sounds shrill and shaky. I try to push past him. He blocks my path.

"I have told you before, if I can't have you, no one can."
His hand cracks across my face. My head snaps back and
I stumble backward. I see red. I flail. I scratch. I kick. I scream.
I fall. When the dust settles, his face is covered with bright red
fingernail marks and we are in a heap, sobbing uncontrolla-
bly. He finally agrees to marriage counseling.

For the next two months we sit across from Dr. Jones
each Saturday morning at 10.

We talk about his anger. My fears. His feelings of emascu-
lation in a marriage where he depends on me financially. He
resents me.

I am sitting in my midtown office when Doctor Jones'
number flashes across the console on my desk. "Hi, Doctor
Jones." My voice is filled with curiosity.

"Hi, Mrs. Hayes." I can hear him typing. "Would you be
able to come to see me this Thursday evening?"

"Sure. But I don't think that Jack—"

"Alone." He cuts me off. "I need you to come alone. It is
my professional opinion that your marriage cannot be saved.
I want to help you to get out."

I secretly begin to see Dr. Jones. I tell him about my childhood in Jamaica. Naomi's accident. The chicken blood inci-
dent. My mother. Michael. Everything. Dr. Jones tells me that
I am living with a sociopath who I empower by taking care
of him. Who lives in a house rent-free and drives my car. Who
seduces me with just enough affection and kindness to keep
me engaged. Dr. Jones begs me to stop clinging to the fantasy
that Jack will change.

"How did I get here?" The wave that has been creeping
toward my eyes pushes through and suddenly I am on the
floor. Rocking.

"You have to leave him." Dr. Jones is kneeling beside me.
He looks at me intently. "Women like you who have had

hellish childhoods and multiple emotional traumas tend to be trusting and kind and nurturing. You are an easy target because men like Jack rely on your decency and brokenness. They tell elaborate lies and heavy sob stories, knowing you don't know how to not care."

"But I am scared to leave. I worry that he will hunt me down and kill me, like those murder-suicide stories I see on TV." My sobs are heavy, and my voice is strangled.

"You are a smart woman. You can do this. Your daughter is away at college now. Save yourself. Sooner than later."

After that session with Dr. Jones, all I can think about is how to leave Jack without becoming a statistic.

On November 3, 2007, coincidentally our wedding anniversary, I am sitting in a Manhattan restaurant having lunch with my friend Isabella. Isabella, a well-respected immigration attorney, was introduced to me nine years earlier by a mutual friend. Although she has a reputation of being a severe and formidable lawyer, when we met for lunch for the first time at a midtown restaurant, I experienced her as an empathetic and warm woman. Her striking blue eyes settled on me as I told her my life stories and at times, she was visibly stunned by some of the things I had experienced. An unlikely friendship was formed that day between a woman from Jamaica, West Indies, and a blonde-haired, blue-eyed woman from Chicago. Our friendship flourished over the years, and she became my confidante, my voice of reason and one of my closest friends.

Almost a decade later, as we dine on Indian cuisine, we are discussing what we always discuss: my husband Jack, and how I can escape him. By the end of lunch, we have a plan. I return to my office, dial Jack's number and set it in motion.

"Hey. What's up, babe?" Jack sounds unusually chipper.

"I have bad news." I listen to his breathing as mine hitches. "My company is transferring me to the Los Angeles office."

"What? What do you mean they are transferring you to L.A.?"

"It's not forever, babe. Just for the next six months to a year." Silence. "I have to sell the house, as I won't be able to pay the rent in California as well as the mortgage and house expenses in Brooklyn."

"Okay. Now what?" I hear the panic in his voice.

"I will help you to find an apartment for you and Cheyenne. When I come back, we will continue working on our marriage."

"Maybe I can come with you?"

"Sure, if you want to." I stifle a giggle. Jack is terrified of and has never been on a plane. In ensuing months, I put the house up for sale and quietly rent and furnish my Upper East Side luxury high-rise apartment that overlooks the East River. I visit it every chance I get, just to sit in the space and enjoy the stillness of my new home. I climb into my queen-size sleigh bed and settle into the gray Egyptian cotton sheets and matching throw pillows. The burgundy leather storage ottoman that sits beneath the large flat screen television that hangs on the wall is stuffed with crisp new sheets and towels. It's a long way from the mice-and cockroach-infested South Bronx apartment of my former father-in-law.

I walk through the living room and feel the excitement rush over me as I take in the sight of my cushy oversized olive-green sofa, bookshelf, a glass center table and large television set. The marble tiled bathroom with the power shower gives my one-bedroom apartment a nice finishing touch of elegance. I amble over to the window and take in what will undoubtedly be my favorite view, the beautiful and calming waters of the East River. I can't wait to wake up daily to this magnificent view.

My friends and family fill their trunks with items that won't be easily missed, and we covertly move them to my new place. Oddly, at times I am gripped with pangs of guilt. The feeling that I am betraying and abandoning my husband after almost two decades together.

Leaving is harder than I expected, and I contemplate staying put in my Brooklyn home, with my unhinged husband and sweet blue-eyed dog. I arrive home early one evening in December 2007 to find Jack frenziedly cleaning the house. I stand and watch him as he mops, dusts and polishes.

"Hey, Jack." I eye him curiously as I place my bag on the sofa and remove a manila folder. "What are you doing?"

"Hey, babe. Just cleaning up a bit." He grins at me as he uses the back of his hand to wipe his forehead. Jack rarely cleans the house.

"I received my offer letter today." I hand him the folder with the offer letter that I drafted on company letterhead.

"Oh?" He leans the mop against the wall, inspects the document and reads aloud: "Human Resources Branch Manager. Flower Drive. Los Angeles. Good for you, babe."

He hands it back to me and resumes mopping before looking up at me with a wide smile. My skin crawls.

January 10, 2008

7:52 a.m.

Jack drives me to the bus stop. "Have a good day, baby." He kisses my cheek.

"You, too." I climb out of the car and board the 8 a.m. Midtown BM-1 Manhattan-bound express bus from Mill Basin. I watch him wave and pull off as I settle into a window seat. I see his car at a red light across the avenue.

What if he doesn't go to work today? What if he calls in sick? What if he forgets something and returns home?

8:15 a.m.

I get off the bus at 23rd Street and quickly hop on the Number 5 train heading back to Brooklyn. I must get home by 9 a.m.

8:48 a.m.

I turn slowly onto our street; my eyes nervously scan the neighborhood for any sign of a Black Acura Legend. I rush into the house and gather the boxes that have been secretly packed and hidden in the backs of closets, under beds and in crevices of the basement. I drag them all into the middle of the living room floor. Cheyenne, our beautiful blue-eyed fur baby, licks my cheeks then studies the flurry of activity from her doggie-bed. I hear a car and I forget how to breathe. I peer through the lavender vertical blinds with dread so thick, I can vomit. My neighbor pulls into his driveway.

Where the hell is my baby sister?

8:58 a.m.

I hear movement in the driveway. My legs wobble. I peek again. The moving truck is backing in. Tears of relief flood my face. I brush them away and rush out to meet the movers.

"Please hurry. Hurry." I try to sound casual. "I have a plane to catch," I lie.

9:20 a.m.

The movers hurry up and down the stairs grabbing the items that I labeled with large yellow Post-its. They seem to be moving in slow motion. I feel as if I am about to take flight from my skin. The doorbell rings and the blood drains from my face. I run upstairs to where the movers are and look out the guest bedroom window. I dash down the stairs, fling the front door open and collapse into my baby sister's arms.

'Where were you? I am so scared that he is going to come back," I bawl.

"It's okay, Dee. Sorry, I got stuck in traffic."

11:07 a.m.

The Flatrate van backs out of my driveway, and I crumble over Cheyenne. I want to take her, but she doesn't belong to me, and my new building doesn't allow large dogs. I lay my head and weep into her soft fur. She nuzzles me with her cold nose and campaigns for a belly rub. I oblige her and gaze into blue eyes that I will never see again.

"Goodbye, Cheyenne. Mommy will always love you." I hand her a snack and give her one last kiss before putting on my coat. I reach the door and turn back to look at the place that I have called home for almost eight years. My big beautiful living room with the long leather sectional, Cheyenne's white fluffy bed with her name embroidered in black lettering, the crystal chandelier and the wedding pictures that line the wall leading up to the bedrooms. I take one last look at Cheyenne whose eyes are locked on me. Her tongue hangs and her breathing is heavy. I run to her for one last hug.

11:13 a.m.

My eyes scan the block one last time as my mind rewinds to the day I fled from my mother in a taxi with Michael. The day I escaped from Michael in a broken-down Chevette with a one-year-old sleeping in the back seat. This will be my last run along these broken roads.

I look up at the blue-green awning and the dried-up potted flowers that hang on either side of the railing below the white mailbox. It all seems so benign from the outside. My body is wracked with sobs for Cheyenne, who I know is standing on the other side of the door with her nose pressed against the floor. Sniffing. Somehow knowing. I take in the hum of my sister's car as we ride in silence toward Manhattan.

I spend the afternoon unpacking my boxes in my beautiful, albeit smaller space. I watch, bewitched and fascinated with the water view of the East River from my apartment and gaze at the caravan of cars that move along the FDR. I remember the first time I saw the Upper East Side. It was in the late 1990s, and Jack and I were returning from dropping off Ava at summer camp in Bear Mountain. We somehow made a detour and found ourselves meandering through the posh residential neighborhood with its upscale high-rises; Gracie Mansion, the home of New York's mayor; and the quaint restaurants and shops. I remember fantasizing about waking up in one of those buildings and walking along streets with such refined character. I could never have imagined myself in such a place. Never in a million years would I have imagined that such a fantasy would come true. I think about the trajectory of my career and how I got here.

Shortly after Michael moved me into his father's rat-invested apartment in 1984, I knew that to get out, we needed extra money. So, each Sunday evening, I would walk to the store to get *The New York Times* and spread the want-ad sections across the bed. I would circle every job I believed that I could possibly do. Data Entry Clerk. Receptionist. File Clerk. Stock Clerk. Customer Service Representative. Then I would make a list of the company, the position and the phone numbers and spend hours standing at the payphone, each Monday morning, dropping in dime after dime, calling number after number, hoping to be invited to interview.

Sometimes, I would get a personnel agency on the line, who was just looking for potential candidates to keep in their databases, and quite often the voice on the other end would say that the job had already been filled. I could taste the disappointment mingled with frustration as I drew a line through those. But sometimes, I would get lucky and someone from an actual company would pick up the phone. One such morning, I reached the hiring manager at Algamene Bank Nederland, a Dutch bank that was in the Wall Street area of Manhattan. He told me to come to the office to fill out an application. I was sitting in the reception area the next morning at 8:30, doing just that. I handed the completed application to the receptionist, who asked me to wait.

I was shaking with excited hope, because I was told that I would fill out the application and leave. Fifteen minutes later, a gray-haired man with a pot belly and a sweaty forehead asked me to follow him. I sat across from him in his cluttered and stuffy office as he studied my application and resume before asking me about my previous places of employment: a receptionist for the Kelly Girl agency and a file clerk in the bursar's office at Hunter College. I explained that I am punctual, a hard worker and have good attention to detail. The next morning at 8:55 a.m., I was standing in front of the bodega down the block, his card in my hand, waiting for 9 a.m., the time he told me to call.

He offers me the bank clerk job. I dialed Michael's job and told him the good news. We were both excited. If we saved, we could be out of his father's house in no time. I left his father's Bronx apartment at 6:30 each morning and boarded the Number 2 train to make it for my 7:30 a.m. start time. I then spent the next one-and-a half hours ripping apart oversized computer- generated reports that left my hands black from the carbon. I would then stack the reports on a large shopping cart and deliver them to each department on the various floors before the staff arrived at 9 a.m. I left at 3:30 p.m., and took the Lexington Avenue line to Hunter College for my 4 p.m. class. My last class ended at 10 p.m.

The hours and the work were grueling, so I quit and took temporary clerical jobs until I became pregnant with Ava and was confined to bed. After she was born, I found a front desk receptionist position at a personnel agency, where I worked for almost seven years. A friend of my mother's invited me to apply for an equity research assistant job that was available at the company where she worked, Prudential Securities. The year was 1992, my daughter was six years old and Jack and I had been together for three years. The offices were fancy and overlooked the South Street Seaport.

Although I didn't really understand the work, and my word-processing skills were pretty poor, my boss was very patient and allowed me to take Word and Excel classes until my work product improved. I was offered the opportunity to sit for my Series 7 and Series 63 certifications, basic broker licenses. Again, I didn't understand any of the material, but each night after Ava was tucked in, I studied and studied until it began to make some sense. I passed the test and became a licensed broker on the second try.

My career in the financial services industry was born. I dial Jack's number.

"Hello?"

"Hi Jack." I close my eyes and sink into my new olive-green couch. "What's up?"

"I moved out of the house today."

"What do you mean, you moved out? I thought you were waiting for a date from your company?"

"My date is today. I didn't tell you because I didn't want any drama. I think it is better this way?"

"I want my marriage." His voice sounds heavy.

"Jack, we'll talk about it when I get back from L.A. Right now, let's just focus on getting the house sold."

"I promise that I will be a better husband, Donna. I have been so stupid and did a lot of crazy things, but I—"

"Jack!" I cut him off. "I am going to send you some money so that you can find an apartment for you and Cheyenne. You should start looking because I think we may have an offer in the coming days."

"Can I see you before you leave?" I hear the urgency in his voice. "Let's go bowling. Just you and me."

Bowling? For the past 19 years you have terrorized and neglected me. Now that I have left, you want to go bowling?!

"I have to catch a flight tonight. But I will call you when I get to L.A. Talk soon."

"Okay. Baby, I love you."

Sure, you do. Now.

"Take care of yourself, Jack." I disconnect the line.

* * *

It is a sunny Saturday afternoon in late August 2008. I walk along East End Avenue after brunch with Isabella. My phone rings.

"Hey, Donna!" My lawyer's voice sounds chipper.

"Hey, Ed! Tell me you have good news for me."

"I do. You are officially homeless. We closed this morning." His laugh is hearty. "That is amazing news." I feel as if a giant brick was just lifted from my chest. "Congratulations, Donna. Go live your life."

I hang up the phone and immediately make two calls: a

divorce lawyer and Verizon Wireless for a new mobile number. I amble along the river past Gracie Mansion toward my apartment. I feel light and wistful. I no longer have my big house. I miss Cheyenne more than words can express. But I am free. I am safe. I am home.

Sixteen

THE LAST WAVE

MY LIFE POST-MARRIAGE IS LIKE BEING DROPPED in a new reality and everything seems shimmery and bright. With Ava safely away at college in Pittsburgh, Pennsylvania, completing her last year at Point Park University, I luxuriate in the freedom and newness of my life on the Upper East Side. There is a buoyancy to my existence. That crippling fear that has lived and danced in the corner of my throat for almost two decades is slowly crawling away. I fall into the sweet chaotic rhythm of life in Manhattan. Long walks through the cool air of Central Park. Sitting on random benches in absolute stillness, absorbing the city's energy. Wandering along produce-perfumed aisles of farmer's markets. Sephora makeovers, just because. I am still healing from the hellish years, so depression visits frequently, and sometimes I unwittingly allow it to lure me back to dark places of self-pity, raging anger and varying states of despondency. I begin therapy and do my best to keep tuned in to all the things that make me happy. Long talks with my daughter, massages, journaling and bubble baths.

It is a Friday evening in the autumn of 2008, and Mama has been on my mind. It has been eighteen years since she passed, but I still think of her. I line the rim of the tub with my favorite accouterments, an assortment of scented candles, a face mask, loofah and eucalyptus body scrub. I pour a generous amount of lavender bubble bath and swirl it around with my hands until the bubbles fill the tub with a luxurious foam and turn off the lights.

The unmistakable floral aroma of lavender seeps into my nostrils and senses. I slide down and sink into the glistening bubbles that tickle my skin. I rest my head against the curve of the tub and slowly begin to relax before I pick up Mama's last letter that I had placed on the toilet lid. I unfold it. It has so many creased lines, from being folded and unfolded. I press the last letter that Mama wrote to me against my face. The paper is soft against my skin and as always, I find comfort in knowing that she once touched it. Held it in her strong hands as she walked in the hot sun toward the post office in town.

My occasional bedtime ritual of reading her letter while immersed in warm sudsy water with candlelight dancing around me is particularly soothing when I feel lonely. Disconnected. I believe that a part of her still lives on in her final words to me. As I gaze at the wobbly shadows that dance against the bathroom wall, my mind drifts to the bedtime of my youth in Jamaica. I would watch the flickering of the dim light from the kerosene lamp, which would cast a circular amber glow across the ceiling. My eyes would get heavy watching the dancing shadows as I waited for her and Dada to stop moving about in the kitchen and come to bed. I turn my attention back to the letter. Although I have it memorized, I like to read it as if it's the first time:

August 3, 1988

Dear Donna,

It was good to hear from you. Thank you for the money that you sent for me. I thank the good Lord for waking me up this morning. Keep asking the good Lord to direct your path and he will keep you. Leave everything in his hands. The blood pressure is not so good, and the old knees are giving me trouble. But I put all my trust in the man above. I hope to see you before the good Lord take me home. As it leaves me nothing else to say, until I hear from you again.

Your grandmother,
Neomina

The buzzing of my cell phone scoops me back. I grab it off the side of the sink. "Hello?"

"Hey, Donna." I hear the voice of my friend Erika.

"Hey, Erika. How are you?" I have known Erika since our children were toddlers. We met when we worked as receptionists for an employment agency and she was a bridesmaid in my wedding to Jack. But we haven't spoken in a while.

"I am doing okay." She pauses before continuing with even more random small talk. "Your godson is getting so big!"

"They grow up so fast, don't they? I can't believe that Ava is twenty-two already," I reply.

"We are getting old, girl." We both giggle. Then more silence.

"I saw Jack today," she blurts out, and the blood drains from my face. I close my eyes and take deep breaths as she continues. "He knows that you are not in California. He has been calling your office every day and just listening to your voice."

I knew it! For the past few months, my office phone rings. I answer. I hear someone breathing.

Then the line goes dead. Repeat.

"I just want you to be careful. He is very angry that you left the way you did. He even asked me if I knew where you live." I gaze at the shadows on the ceiling and I am now surprisingly calm. Uncharacteristically unaffected.

"I told him I don't. But please be careful."

I thank her and assure her that I will be alright, before sinking back into the tub, allowing the sensation of the warm water to calm me. I have often wondered what I would do if and when he finds out that I never left New York. More importantly, what would he do? I surrender to my imagination: Brown eyes, hidden behind dark shades, squint at me from the supermarket's entrance as I push my cart of groceries along the produce aisle, blissfully unaware of the closeness of my volatile ex-husband. His tall lanky frame blends into the rush hour crowd and lingers behind me as I make my way down the subway stairs. He plants himself at the opposite end of the subway car, his cold unwavering gaze boring into me. Across the street from my office and apartment buildings, he studies me.

Maybe he'll just hang back, puff on a cigarette and glare through wisps of curling dancing smoke. Or maybe he'll approach me with gritted teeth and clenched fists, a burning rage hissing through his body to threaten me. Attack me.

But in this moment, I choose peace and disallow the familiar feeling of dread to assault me. I close my eyes and inhale then exhale deeply, as the scent of lavender fills my nose. *In. Out. In. Out.*

"Mama, I know that you are watching over me from heaven, and I am going to be just fine." I kiss her letter and return it to the top of the toilet seat cover.

I step out of the tub and wrap my robe around me. I feel the cool tile against my damp feet as I move across the floor to the kitchen to brew a cup of peppermint tea.

Propped up on a barstool by the living room window, my hands cup the warmth of my tea mug and I hum along to Norah Jones' "Don't Know Why" that plays on my phone. I get lost in the lyrics. Music is and has always had a powerful calming effect on me. The soundtrack of my life. Neil Diamond's "Sweet Caroline" reminds me of the summer of 1971 when the trees swayed in the warm breeze and my sisters and I chased butterflies with pretty wings of yellow and black, or jumped rope until dusk.

We sang along to the chorus that blared from Dada's transistor radio that was perched on the ledge of the red veranda. The Third Degrees' "When Will I See You Again?" takes me back to my first year at Westwood, when the whimsical, almost anthem-like chorus was a delight to sing at the top of our lungs each time it made it onto the airwaves. Fat Joe's "What's Love Got to Do with It?" elicits a memory of riding in the car with Jack when we sang and bobbed our heads to the beat, the music uniting us, if only temporarily.

While I lived in Brooklyn, I belonged to a performing arts group that I joined at the age of forty when Ava left for college. Open mics and performances were nerve-wracking, yet beautifully exciting. Music is my happy place, my language, my solace and trusty companion that prompted the childhood concerts for the chickens, dogs and the pretty flowers in Mama's garden. My raised voice in high-school choruses, the church choir and years of college theatre performances at Hunter College. I miss singing and performing.

The East River looks like shiny black glass shimmering under the moonlight. I sit in the stillness and take in the brilliant stars that fill the sky then turn my attention to the planes that cross the evening sky to and from JFK and LaGuardia. The "Nearness of You" flows from my iPhone and fills the air, rushing in and around me. I sing along as I enter my bedroom, which is bathed in dim lighting from the two lamps on the night tables. As I settle under the blanket and give thanks for another day, I feel the need to resume what comes naturally to me. Singing.

A Google search of singing classes on the Upper East Side leads me to the lobby of the cultural center of the 92nd Street Y to audition for a cabaret class. I step out of the January chill and enter the hustle and bustle of the spacious lobby and check my phone for the audition room. Nervousness mingled with excitement buzz around in my belly. I am greeted by the cabaret director, a tall woman with a warm smile and short brown hair that she constantly pushes behind her ear.

"Hi, Donna. So nice to meet you." We shake hands and she motions to a row of chairs. "You can put your things over there."

"Hi. Thanks for inviting me to audition." I smile and place my bag and coat on one of the gray folding chairs and follow her to the stage.

"This is our musical director." A small-framed woman with silver-rimmed glasses perched on the bridge of her nose is seated stage right behind a grand piano. She stands and shakes my hand.

"Hi, Donna. Welcome. What will you be singing for us today?" she asks, adjusting her glasses upward. I hand her the sheet music to "A Time for Us" from *Romeo and Juliet*, and she plays the intro. The jitters cause my hands to shake as I swim in the lyrics of the first verse, then the bridge. By the second verse, I feel transcendent. The vibrations of the piano make my skin all tingly as that familiar sense of freedom that only the stage can offer fills me. Days later, I receive my acceptance email; before long I am immersed in the New York cabaret scene. What follows is a rebirth in every way. I sing to packed rooms and bow to thunderous applause. I have a publicist, a band and fan emails. It feels like a lifetime ago when rats circled my bed. When food was scarce. When I cowered in the shower as Jack ranted on the other side of the bathroom door before cracking it with his fist.

Three years after that cabaret audition and numerous concerts, I sing the finale to close my fourth solo show. The audience honors me with a standing ovation, and I bathe in the purple haze of the stage lights and generous applause. I take several bows before stepping off the stage and moving toward the back of the room. Shadowy figures. Smiling. Clapping. I feel blessed to be here. Doing what I love more than anything else on the planet.

I walk toward the front of the theatre and sit on one of the pastel-colored benches in the foyer and gaze at the traffic crawling along 22nd Street. Tonight's set was alive and magical, and I left my emotions on the stage neatly wrapped in my encore selection of John Lennon's in "In My Life." I savor the moment in quiet reflection and think of the stumbles and string of events that led me here. My husband's abandonment, abuse and betrayal left me no choice but to dig deep and find the will to run, bruised and broken, toward a better life. I have proven to myself that I can overcome any obstacle. Gone is the fragile little girl who waited for someone to save her. I had to save myself. I smile at the irony of the role that adversity played in the creation of my new life. The pain that these men inflicted on me, gave me the courage to create a better life for myself. The chatter of the club's patrons snaps me back to the club's foyer. I walk toward the line that is already forming.

One by one they tell me how much they enjoyed my singing and how inspired they were by my life stories. Tonight, I had told the audience about my mechanic angel who fixed my car for free as I tried to escape from Michael with a one-year-old. My high school bullies who stalked me along the shiny hallways of my high school, and stories of my childhood in Jamaica with Mama. I study their faces, bright with enthusiasm and excitement. Such post-performance attention always feels unnecessary and overly triumphal, but I am humbled by the overwhelming support, nevertheless.

Two men are standing off to the side near the bar. One is crying and the other, who is wearing a Barney-colored purple suit and oversized black glasses, appears to be comforting him. I know I should focus on the people in front of me, vying for my attention, but I am drawn to these men. Crying Man starts speaking. I shift my body and tilt my ear with subtlety.

"Her performance of 'Lies of Handsome Men' just broke my heart," he says as he dabs the corner of his eyes with napkins from the bar counter. I feel them watching me as I accept flowers and kiss the cheeks of the givers. "The lyrics and her commitment to the story was just so moving," Crying Man continues. I punt my attention between those on the receiving line and the conversation between the two men.

"I know. It was a beautiful show indeed," says Purple Suit Man. "She is doing this show again next week and I will be right here," he adds.

"Well, if I wasn't going back to Wisconsin on Sunday, I would be right here as well. She is a wonderful singer and a great storyteller," replies Crying Man, as Purple Suit Man nods in agreement. They get on the back of the line and before long, are standing in front of me. They tell me that they enjoyed the show and ask for a picture. We pose with glowing smiles before they walk out into the night air to hail a cab.

I am humbled by the words they don't know that I heard. Words I will forever hold close. Their cab pulls off and I turn back to my fans with a full heart and a clear view of what I believe to be my life's purpose. To use my life stories to inspire, to motivate and encourage.

They need not be in vain.

My life is rebooting nicely. I book a few bit and background roles on television shows: *Orange Is the New Black,* and *Law and Order: SVU,* reenactment shows on the Discovery and Biography channels. I perform my one-woman shows and my decades-long Wall Street career continues to flourish. I now realign my life as an active participant in it and not a victim of all the horror that happened. I want the thrilling adventures and the challenges to continue, so my 2011 new year's resolution is to run, something that I haven't done since Westwood.

Four months before my 49th birthday, I join the New York Road Runners (NYRR) club beginner's running class. Our first run is on a frigid January evening and the wind is wild. We sidestep icy patches as we move along the running path in Central Park. We run one minute. We walk two. I hyperventilate. My lungs burn. But I show up each week, dressed in my color-coordinated running gear complete with thick mittens and hand warmers, until I can run for thirty minutes without stopping. I get stronger. I get leaner. I run a few 5K's. Then a 10K. Then a half-marathon.

I stand in the last wave, the slowest group in the 2014 New York City Marathon. I am fifty-two years old. As I look around at the mass of runners, I still find it hard to believe that I qualified to run.

I had been overweight and out of shape for most of my adult life. During my childhood in Jamaica, I was alarmingly thin. I ate because I had to and not because I derived any particular pleasure from it, except for the occasional sweet treats. However, when I migrated to the United States, my addiction to food began. The abundance of donuts, chips and candy was overwhelming. Very soon food became my greatest comfort and my body thickened, which worsened during the seven months that I remained in bed during my pregnancy with Ava. My addiction to food lingered and comforted me throughout my marriages—when I was anxious, sad, terrified or lonely. Living in or near low-income neighborhoods offered greater access to an abundance of cheap food sources, and so I indulged and overindulged in the salty, sugary, and deep-fried foods. The $1 menu and other value meals from McDonalds and other fast-food chains became a staple in my diet when that was all I could afford. The burgers, fries, apple pies and hash browns that I lathered with grape jelly are cheap and convenient. I immersed myself on a journey of mindless emotional eating that offered the numbness that I needed to move through those stages of my life.

My weight ballooned, and I forced my body into a size twenty-two dress to celebrate my forty-second birthday. I couldn't walk up a flight of stairs without gasping, and wore a heart monitor to track palpitations. I hated my body. Unlike Michael, who moved in with his mistress because of my weight gain, not once had Jack complained or made me feel unattractive because of my weight. I often wonder if that, in any way, influenced my decision to stay with him for nineteen years. In 2004, I joined Weight Watchers and hired a personal trainer. It took a year, but I dropped 70 pounds and slipped into a size 6. I feel very proud to stand amid a crowd of marathoners as we prepare to run 26.2 miles.

I pull my red Nike hat tightly over my ears as the wind drags its icy fingers along my back.

"I am freezing!" I whine to Charlotte, my beautiful Trinidadian running coach, and my 60-year-old friend and running partner, Kenneth. We all met on the first day of running class, three years earlier. "I never thought I would ever say this, but I can't wait to start running just to warm up."

"Slow and easy," Charlotte warns as she stretches her arms above her head.

"I can't believe that I am doing this a second time," Kenneth chimes in and shakes his head in disbelief. We all laugh and jump around in place to keep warm. Kenneth tucks a tuft of blond hair under his blue-green wool hat, which accentuates his freakishly blue eyes. For the past four months, Kenneth, Charlotte and I have trained in almost every corner of Central Park. We have pushed ourselves through countless miles, in nasty weather, over hills, along the reservoir and up the dreaded steepness of Harlem Hill. All in preparation for this day. This moment.

The gun blares and we move across the start. I gape at the grandness of the Verrazano Bridge as we push against the wind. I feel in-over-my-head but try to focus on the exciting energy around me as I self-talk.

Breathe in through your nose and out your mouth. It's about the journey.

One step at a time. Breathe.

I distract myself by studying the cadence of the stronger runners and the beautiful NYC skyline. We move through Brooklyn then Queens. We resort to power walking and running intervals as the vastness of the Queensboro Bridge beckons. My body wants to give up, but we climb side by side. Pushing. Panting. We exit the bridge at mile 16. The roar of the First Avenue crowd warms me. Charlotte runs ahead.

Too spent to talk, Kenneth and I smile feebly at each other. It is now a mental game. We run, walk, run, walk toward the Willis Avenue Bridge in the Bronx. Silently I recite my mantras and listen to the playlist I painstakingly created for this day. I try to think positive thoughts, but my brain is foggy.

It is dusk when Kenneth and I start the last three miles over the rolling hills of Central Park. We have been running/walking for almost six hours. *It's not a race. You just have to finish.*

As I move through the darkness of Central Park, I decide to think of all the things that I have to be grateful for. For the amazing life that I have fought so hard for and get to live each day. For all my former co-workers at my receptionist job who stopped at supermarkets on their way to the office and bought groceries for me at a time when I had no money for food to feed my two-year old, after her father left us. For the analyst who referred me for my first human resources generalist job. The colleagues who referred me to the executive at Salomon Smith Barney who at the time, did not have any openings, but hired me anyway as a floater.

Within weeks I had my own job as a human resources recruiter and then human resources generalist. Forever grateful to my manager who left Salomon Smith Barney to join my current company and offered me a position on her team as an assistant vice president. Within a few years, I was promoted to vice president and then director. Twenty-three years later, I am a managing director and deputy head of human resources for the Americas.

My heart swells with gratitude, and tears come, but I am too tired to wipe them away.

I see the Mile 25 sign. My legs feel as if they are encased in cement. Kenneth is staring straight ahead as we move through the darkness of Central Park. The landscape of runners is now very sparse. Long gone is the throng of runners who surrounded us at the start in Staten Island. Two couples are ahead of us. A lone man hobbles behind us. Another couple staggers behind him. We all push against something invisible. I don't feel my legs anymore as I run on empty. My mind is in frenzied chaos. I just want to stop moving.

The sound of our shuffling feet against the pavement strangles the stillness. Is the finish line still there?

What if everyone went home?

We round the bend at Columbus Circle when I hear it. Faint at first, but I am pretty sure it is cheering. My emotions pile up and cascade down my frozen cheeks. I see banners. The cheering is louder now. Two women stand in the shadows clanging cowbells and offering words of encouragement. *You can do it. Almost there. Congratulations. You just ran a fucking marathon!* Resurgence. We pick up the pace and push. Panting and spent, we cross the finish line—26.2 miles. It feels as if a permanent smile has been etched in my face. Someone places a medal around my neck and hands me a cup of Gatorade.

"I did it, Charlotte! Kenneth, I just ran a fucking marathon!" We all hug.

"You should be so proud of yourself, Donna!" Kenneth smiles at me. "That wind was no joke."

I groan in agreement as we sip Gatorade and head out of the park draped in silver heat sheets with our medals dangling from our necks. Frozen and triumphant.

Two weeks later, my fifth cabaret show, "Ordinary Miracles," debuts at the Metropolitan Room. I wear a sleek black dress with bell sleeves and my marathon medal around my neck. I tell more personal stories about perseverance and resilience and victories and losses. I weave in songs by Billie Holiday and U2 and Nancy Wilson. The Metropolitan Room offers me an artist in residency contract. For the first time in my life, I feel present and in control of my life. No longer a spectator. Ever since I completed the marathon two weeks earlier, the high from the race lingers.

The confidence that I feel from going from obese to marathon runner bleeds into other areas of my life. I strut about my life feeling confident. There is nothing that I cannot accomplish.

I wake and get all gussied up before starting my day. I grab my grande sugar-free hazelnut soy extra hot latte at

Starbucks and enter a very elegant building in Midtown Manhattan to play the role of executive. Some nights I sing or play characters on dimly lit stages in theatres.

However, after the applause, late dinner meetings or business trips to Europe, I come home and settle into the silence of my apartment, which I still love very much. With my false lashes atop my vanity and my suit or sequined dress hung up, the stillness is an acute reminder of the gaping void that still lives inside of me. I am in my early fifties, and I have been in only two relationships—two scar-inducing marriages. I often gaze at the cars from my window as they move along the FDR and dream of a day when I will sit in the passenger side and watch the road with my beloved as we travel to places where lovers go and do what lovers do.

As my fifty-fourth birthday looms, I want more than ever to experience just one relationship that is not abusive or dysfunctional. I want my own human. My 2016 New Year's Resolution is to give internet dating a try. I meet Javier De Leon two weeks later on Our Time.

Seventeen

OPEN HOUSE

JAVIER AND I START THE TWO-HOUR DRIVE to Waterbury, Connecticut, on a cool crisp Sunday morning to see the house almost two months after our one-year anniversary dinner. A pristine blanket of white hugs the landscape following yesterday's snowfall. Branches hang low under the weight of the snow as we cruise along I-95. I recline my seat and gaze through the sunroof at the sun filtering through the cottony clouds.

"Baby wake up. We are here." Javier touches my shoulder and I open my eyes and look around sleepily.

"Where is the house?" I press the button on the side and adjust my seat to an upright position to look around. We are cruising through a sleepy neighborhood.

"We are not there yet," he responds as he points out a church, a pool hall, a restaurant and a gym. "I just want you to see the neighborhood."

Ten minutes later, Javier pulls up to a teal-colored three-story house that is surrounded by tall weeds and debris. I look around at the neighborhood houses with their bay windows and chimneys and drawn curtains and picket fences.

A stray cat ambles by and disappears around a corner. Javier fumbles with his cousin's keys. I gaze at an abandoned red and black Trans Am that is parked off to the side of the house.

Javier tries key after key for almost ten minutes before the front door finally opens and we are standing in the foyer of a shell of a house. The air is thick with staleness and mildew. He opens the door to the first floor. It is the smallest of three apartments. Two bedrooms and one bathroom. It is strewn with buckets, shovels, empty paint cans, brushes, brooms and large garbage containers.

"Babe, all the windows are new," Javier explains, as he takes my hand and leads me to the second floor. He shows me where the bedrooms, bathrooms, laundry room and kitchen would be. We get to the top floor and Javier can barely contain his excitement.

"Baby, this would be our floor." He flails his arms excitedly. "It has five bedrooms and three bathrooms." He scurries to the other end of the floor. "Look over here. This could be your office." He frames the space with his hand as his voice echoes in the hollowness. He steps through a framed doorway to another area and directs my attention to a space below a large window. "This is the laundry room." He then moves to the other corner and continues his staging: "Two guest bedrooms are over here for when your daughter or my sons visit."

He turns to look at me. "What do you think, baby?"

"It has a lot of potential." I smile at my love. I don't really *love* it, but maybe I have become a snob after living in Manhattan for almost ten years. I look around the cavernous space and self-talk.

It's not so bad, Donna.

After all, you will be retired and won't have to commute daily, and Javier can drive you into the city for auditions and appointments.

You may not love it now, but after it's fixed up, it will be our gorgeous castle. I love the idea that this would be a home that we could build together.

Javier guides me through the debris toward the window on the other side of the room. "Baby, look at this view!" He stands behind me and wraps his arms around my waist.

The view is breathtaking. I lean against him and study the skyline in the distance. "So peaceful."

"Javier, this is a gorgeous view," I admit. "I just can't understand why your cousin has kept this house vacant for eight years."

"He has some financial issues, but now that he is getting married, he really needs the money," he says dismissively. "I spoke with him this morning when I picked up the keys and he is willing to sell it to you for $70,000—if you decide you want to buy it, that is."

Before I could process that information, he is leading me down an iron staircase that is twisted in a perfect spiral. Decorating ideas of overstuffed couches, floor lamps, candles and duvet covers are dancing in my head. I find myself imagining retirement in Waterbury, Connecticut. It is no Manhattan. But it is more economical. A decent apartment in Manhattan is at least $600,000, which would require a mortgage. This just makes more sense financially.

We get to the bottom of the staircase and enter a massive basement. "I will fix it up real nice down here, and this is where the super would live." He pushes out his chest and sticks out his chin.

"Okay, Mr. Superman. Calm down. We are not there yet." I study his smile and his brown eyes that dart from side to side as he points out the size of the basement, big enough for a gym and a pool table. He is so adorable when he is excited. I smile at my love. His enthusiasm is contagious.

Waterbury, Connecticut, is known for the beautiful Palace Theatre and Seven Angels Theatre. Maybe I will audition for one of their musical productions. Javier and I will picnic or walk along the trails of the Hop Brook Lake. We'll take walking tours of the Bank Street Historic District. Yes. Javier and I could have a great life in Waterbury, Connecticut.

He opens the back door that leads to a vast backyard which is completely blanketed by snow. My excitement is beginning to match Javier's as I watch him step out into the backyard and trudge through the crunchy snow to look around. I imagine a garden like Mama's or sitting under the large tree with a book. Maybe even a pool. Even if I decide not to live here, it would be a steady rental income after I retire.

I must admit that it has a lot of potential.

We chatter excitedly on the drive back into the city about rental income, contractors, appliances, decorating ideas, the deed and a renovation schedule. He would stay at the Connecticut house during the week to be the on-site super and spend the weekends with me at my apartment on the Upper East Side. We will split the rental income. We arrive in Manhattan with a solid plan.

Eighteen

ROMANTIC GETAWAY PICNIC

FOR THE NEXT TEN WEEKS, we swirl around in frenzied activity. Javier's family-friend-contractor agrees to give us a break on the price if we pay him in cash. After almost thirty years of working, I take money from my 401K for the first time. I withdraw $50,000, the maximum amount allowed, and combine it with a Discover loan and money from my savings. I am usually a methodical planner, a woman who weighs the pros and cons, who consults with friends and family about major decisions, who has been accused of being overly cautious. Never, ever have I ever been this impulsive about my hard-earned money. Our plans are scary but thrilling at the same time—because I am doing it all with the man I love.

Javier moves into my apartment and our lives begin to blend. We are both very busy. While he oversees the renovations, I land two acting gigs in Phoenix and Los Angeles, while balancing my human resources job at the bank.

"So how is it going in L.A.?" Javier asks one Monday night in late March during one of our nightly chats.

'It's going okay, babe. Tiring, but okay. How are things going with you?"

"I miss you, *chica*." He sighs.

"I miss you, too, baby. So how are the renovations coming along?"

"It's coming. We are finally done with the sheetrock. The plumber and the electrician are coming next week. I think we are going to be on schedule for the June first move-in date."

"So how does it look?" I ask.

"It is beautiful, baby. You are going to love it," he gushes.

"Oh, Javier. I can't wait to see it," I reply, flopping back on the hotel's king-size bed.

"Two of the workers annoyed me today, though," he grumbles.

"Why? What happened, baby?" I ask, staring at the ceiling fan.

"They get a half-hour break to eat or talk or do whatever they want to. Yet they are developing this nasty habit of being on their phones when they are supposed to be working. I was not very happy today and they know it. Believe me, they know it!" he snarls.

"It's okay, baby. Don't let stuff like that get to you." I change the subject. "Let's talk about something pleasant. Tell me more about my retirement home." I close my eyes and listen to his voice.

"Well, my love. All premium materials will be used on the top floor. Our floor. The marble-tiled tub, those fluorescent light fixtures that you want above the kitchen island and the granite tub are all ordered. Oh! And I found the perfect spot for your piano," he adds with excitement.

"Excellent! What else. I want more. More!" I giggle.

"Uh, the landscaper came today. We are putting in a pretty garden for you. I know how much you love flowers that remind you of your grandmother," he chuckled.

"Really? That's great, babe. I want it in the little area below the window facing the ... "

"The front. I know, I know," he interrupted. "You want it to be the first thing you see when you come home. Well your wish is my command, *chica!*" he giggled in my ear.

"Remind me to get gloves, pruners and a pretty sun hat for when I work in my pretty new garden." We both laughed as a childhood image of Mama fills my brain. She is on her knees; her large beige straw hat shades her face from the sweltering sun. Her hands move rapidly, yanking weeds and watering the flowers. Colors are everywhere. Subtle pinks. Purples. Orange. Vibrant reds. The sun bounces off the wet petals, causing them to glow.

"And *why* can't you send me a picture?" I ask with a whine.

"*Chica*, I already told you. It is not at a point where I want you to see it yet. I want you to see the finished product with your beautiful naked eyes." He sounds serious.

"But Javier, I want to—"

"Please, *chica*, for me?" he interrupts. "I want to be standing by your side and looking at your beautiful happy face when you see it for the first time. Please let me do this for you. That would mean the world to me."

"Okay. Fine," I grumble.

"I will send you one picture. Okay?" He laughs.

"Great! Okay." I giggle.

He sends a picture of two birds walking across the lawn with the caption: Look at two love birds walking on the property of two love birds. *Goodnight, chica.*

Three weeks later while we are having dinner in a neighborhood diner on a Sunday evening, he tells me that his mother has been rushed to NYU Medical Center. She is very ill and on a ventilator and he is waiting to hear from the doctor. I try to probe, but he doesn't want to talk about it. He says it depresses him. He just wants to think positively and hope for the best. I attempt to cheer him up as he pushes his pasta dish from one side of the plate to the other.

"Baby, come on, eat your food. It's gonna be ok."

He doesn't. I try something else. "I can't believe that the house will be done by this weekend!" I say, changing the subject.

"I know, *chica*." His face lights up and he reaches his hand across the table and squeezes mine. "Thank you for believing in me and for taking a chance on me. This could not have happened without you. I love you so much."

"I love you too, baby," I reply, feeling giddy with happiness.

The following morning, we cruise along Fifth Avenue and I gaze at the sunlight filtering through the trees. A gentle breeze flutters leaves along the cobblestone path outside Central Park. Our lighthearted Monday morning routine of silly banter and blaring reggaeton is replaced by Javier's uncharacteristic silence. He is stone-faced as he weaves in and out of rush hour traffic.

"Is everything okay, babe? Is it your mom?" I ask, trying to sound nonchalant.

"*Chica!* I already told you. I am fine." There it was again. That unfamiliar trace of aloofness. I take a deep breath and force a smile.

"Are you sure you are alright?" I press. "You are acting a little weird this morning."

He stretches his lips into a faint smile as his hand drifts across to the passenger side and settles in mine.

"I am okay, baby. I promise." He flashes me a quick grin and pats my hand. I feel better instantly. I think about our unlikely love story and what we have managed to accomplish in the sixteen months that we have been together. New rental property in Waterbury, Connecticut. In the coming days, we will be very busy, interviewing potential tenants, conducting credit and background checks, preparing leases and handling last-minute details in preparation for our tenants' June first move-in date.

He pulls into a parking spot across from the JP Morgan Chase branch on Fifty-First Street, turns off the ignition, and faces me.

"I love you, *chica.*" He squeezes my hand. Harder than usual. "Don't worry about me. I'm okay. I am just worried about my mom. She got emphysema from all those years of smoking. I begged her to stop." His voice is heavy.

"We'll get through this together, babe." I try to sound upbeat as I kiss the side of his face and grab my purse. I exit the car and hurry across the street to the bank.

I walk up to the teller window, hoping that Sophia, the branch manager who helped me with the two previous withdrawals, will have time to help me again this morning. I wave at her as she enters the teller station from a side door.

"Another withdrawal today?" She smiles at me from behind the thick glass.

"Yup!" I grin with excitement, as I fill out the withdrawal slip and hand it to her. I swipe my debit card, enter my PIN and slide my card through the opening. Sophia studies the screen and makes notes on my deposit slip. She then places several large stacks of cash into an electronic bill counter, which makes a whirring sound.

Soon Sophia and I are seated in one of the Chase Private Client offices off to the side around a large wooden table counting stacks of $100 bills, a similar scene to the ones in March and April, when we counted eighty-five-thousand dollars in cash.

Up until then, I had never seen that much cash, except on television. The experience is fascinating. Sophia separates the money and hands me a stack of one thousand hundred-dollar bills. I know the drill and begin to count. The bills feel smooth and crisp against my hands. They even have that new money smell.

Excitement is brewing in my belly as I think of what this all represents. The new life that Javier and I are about to embark on together. Our new home.

"So, is the house almost finished? I think you said you guys started the construction in March. Right?" Sophia studies me, her hands moving rapidly. Each bill drops on a growing bundle which she secures with a rubber band.

"Yes. Actually, it will be done this weekend. We are getting ready to interview tenants."

"Congratulations and good luck with everything." She shoots me a wide grin as she stuffs the cash into an oversized JP Morgan Chase envelope. "I want to see pictures."

"Thank you, Sophia, for all your help. I promise to stop by with pictures." I wave at her as I hurry toward the exit and through the revolving door onto Fifty-First Street. Javier is on the phone but hangs up and smiles at me as I slide into the passenger seat.

"That was the doctor. I am going to stop by the hospital before I head to Connecticut."

"How is your mom?" I hand him the envelope that bulges with the $29,000 in cash that Sophia stuffed inside, bringing my total investment to $162,000. For our home. Our new life.

I watch him tuck the envelope under the bottom of his seat as he had done the other two times. He straightens up and pulls me into a giant hug before pulling back. "She's about the same." His eyes are teary. "You are everything to me, *chica*. You have changed my life in a way I could never have imagined." He holds my face in his hands and tilts his head from side to side, the way a dog does when curious or confused. "Thanks for taking a chance on me. On us. I will forever love you. I am so excited about our future together."

My heart warms and I smile lovingly at him. He starts the car and merges into traffic that moves west on Fifty-First Street, turns right onto Sixth Avenue and parks in front of my office building. He steps out, opens the front passenger door, extends his hand and helps me to my feet. He holds my face close to his. His eyes settle in mine before he plants a feathery kiss on my lips. "I'll call you as soon as I get to Connecticut. Okay, *chica*? Have a beautiful day! I love you."

"I love you, too, baby."

He climbs into the driver's seat and pulls off. He waves and turns left onto Fifty-Third Street and I watch the car disappear behind the Hilton Hotel.

Later that night I pack for our weekend stay at the new house. I am beyond excited that I am finally going to see it after two months of renovations. It was Javier's suggestion that we spend the weekend in the empty house. I love the idea. He wants us to be the first ones to spend the night there—to enjoy its newness. He calls it our romantic getaway picnic. I pack my iPad, two sleeping bags, pillows, an overstuffed picnic basket, candles, toiletries, towels and board games. I can't wait to soak in the Jacuzzi tub, cook on the island in the new kitchen and watch the sunset with my beloved from the top floor.

Javier doesn't call on Monday night. He sends texts. He thinks that he is coming down with the flu—fever, sore throat, and all. He says it is difficult for him to talk. He just wants to sleep.

No word from him on Tuesday.

He calls on Wednesday. The call is short, cold, and distant. He tells me that his mother is getting worse, and he is depressed. Thursday morning, at 9:43 a.m., my phone pings the arrival of a text.

"Donna!!! My mother passed away last night. I am extremely emotional. My sisters are falling apart, and I am finding it hard to be strong for them. We can text, but I am too emotional to talk."

My heart breaks for him. I want to be with him, but he doesn't call or pick up when I do.

His mother's wake is on a warm Saturday afternoon at 3 p.m. He sends me a text with a picture of her in her coffin. She is dressed in white lace and her hands are crossed over her chest. Light blue rosary beads wrap around and dangle from her hands. I want to be with him, but he won't answer the phone. I toy with the idea of taking an Uber to the funeral home in the Bronx, but I don't know where it is. He sends me a text explaining that he did not invite me because he is ashamed of the dinky funeral home, the drug-infested neighborhood and the hysteria of his two sisters. He would prefer that I don't come.

I tell him that I understand, but I really don't. I have met one of his sisters and his niece. I have Face-Timed with his mom and his son at least once a month. It's not like I am a complete stranger—but I am not brokenhearted. I don't care for bad neighborhoods, and funerals are depressing. I just want my baby to be okay.

In future texts he proclaims his undying love for me and begs me to be patient with him as he grieves for his mother. He tells me that a young single woman, a married couple and a family of five have signed leases and are now occupying the three floors of my new property. A property that I have yet to see. He promises to stop by with all the paperwork in a few days.

Who are the tenants? Where did he find them? When did he find them? I leave voicemails asking him to call me.

My birthday falls on Mother's Day ten days later. I spend the day on the couch, clinging to optimism and aching to hear his voice. Giving him space to mourn but hoping that our lives will return to normal soon. Another week goes by with no word from Javier. My heart is in shreds.

Two weeks later I have foot surgery. He does not call or show up to take me home as he had promised.

It's now early June, and it has been a month since his mother's death. I haven't seen him since the cool May morning that he drove me to the bank to withdraw the final payment. I am in dreadful pain physically and emotionally. I need him. I ignore his wish to be left alone to grieve, and dial his number. It goes straight to voicemail. I text him and demand an explanation. He writes back and accuses me of being selfish because I won't let him grieve in peace. I ask him to send me all the paperwork, my portion of the rental income and security deposits. His response cracks my soul.

Monday, June 5, 2017
9:07 p.m.
Javier De Leon

Dearest Donna. I realize that you may not be feeling well after your surgery and probably not in the best of moods, but I am certainly not in the mood to discuss how you are entitled to any money, just because you say so. You gave me the money as a gift, so please stop the nonsense and leave me alone.

My face freezes as I stare unblinkingly at his text in utter confusion. I read and re-read the words. Over and over again.

What does he mean by a gift? Is he joking?

Leave me alone? Wait. Is he breaking up with me?

I am sure that he is just crazy with grief because of his mother's death. Maybe he doesn't want to be bothered because he is so sad. But I don't understand what he means by a gift!

My brain is scrambling, trying to make sense of it all. I write him back, but he doesn't answer. My calls go straight to voicemail. I send an email. No response. I try something that I am pretty sure will trigger a response. I threaten to sue him and his cousin, because the money was no gift. I wait a day. No response.

I want to call his family, but I don't have a phone number. I think of all the times that I Face-Timed with his mother, but we always talked on Javier's phone. It never occurred to me to get his mother's number. That poor woman. I can still see her face staring back at me from the other side of his iPhone. Thick eyebrows. Long curly black hair. A sweet, kind voice. May she rest in peace. I wait another day. Nothing.

I enter his sister's name into my Google Browser. Lucia De Leon is a very common name, but if I find her number, maybe she can explain Javier's odd behavior. I am sure she would talk to me. Six months earlier, on a chilly Sunday afternoon in December, Javier drove her home to her apartment in Manchester, Connecticut, and Javier asked me to ride with them.

Although it was my first time meeting Lucia, we hit it off immediately. During the two-hour drive, we sang and bobbed our heads to the reggae and R&B music that filled the car. We talked about Uggs, our children and false eyelashes, and what a cute couple her brother and I made.

Later that evening, I met her daughter and treated them all to dinner at a local diner. We agreed to get together the next time she is in the city. I can't find Lucia's number. Isabella suggests that I contact a lawyer.

Bill Brewster, a Connecticut-based lawyer, sends demand letters to Javier and his cousin, threatening to sue them. I dial Bill's number on a Friday morning, three days after the letters were sent. I need an update. He tells me that Javier called and taunted him after he received the letter. Giggling and challenging him to prove his claims that I gave him any money. Bill told him to come up with the money or be fully prosecuted by the law. Javier tells Bill that if I sue him, he will go public with negative information about me, even if he has to make it up—then laughs and hangs up the phone.

That is not an accurate depiction of the Javier that I know. Maybe he is just having some sort of a mental breakdown because of his mother's death. They were so very close.

Three days later, I call Bill again. "Hey, Bill."

"Hello, Ms. Hayes. Have you heard from De Leon or his cousin?"

"No, I haven't. I can't believe this!"

"I know this is a very difficult situation. This man is pond scum!" Bill replies.

"You know what, Bill? I've been thinking. Maybe he is having some sort of a nervous breakdown, because his mother died a little over a month ago. He has always been a wonderful and devoted boyfriend." Bill remains quiet on the other end as I continue. "Anyway, I had major foot surgery about a week ago, so I can barely stand. It will be a while before I can get to the house to meet the tenants. But I am sure there is a logical explanation for Javier's odd behavior. This is just not him!" I ramble.

"Well, the house is not far from my office. It would take me about 30 minutes. I would be happy to take a drive down to check it out. I can swing by around three this afternoon if you'd like."

"Would you? That would be so great, Bill. Please check on the tenants for me, because he is probably not responding to them either. Please give them my contact information." I am practically shaking with anxiety.

"Ms. Hayes, I will call you as soon as I get there."

"Thanks, Bill. I really appreciate this." I hang up the phone and burst into tears. Partly from my bandaged foot that throbs in pain, and from confused frustration.

I grab my phone on the first ring. "Hi, Bill." Fear crawls around inside of me, as if searching for someplace to settle.

"Hi, Ms. Hayes. I am going to send you some pictures that I took of the house." Long pause.

Deep breaths.

"The house has not been renovated, and there are no tenants."

The lump that has taken up residence in my throat roars to the surface and I crumble in uncontrollable sobs. My mind is decimated as I pummel Bill with questions. "Are you sure that you went to the right address? Are you sure? Maybe the tenants aren't home—" My voice trails off mid-sentence. My throat is dry and raw. I can't locate my breath.

"Ms. Hayes. Ms. Hayes. Try to calm down." Bill's voice sounds so far away.

"What's happening? I don't understand. I just don't understand." I can only muster a whisper.

"Ms. Hayes, unfortunately you have been the victim of a romance scam. Nothing Javier De Leon told you about the house is true. I am sending over pictures."

His words sail at me missile-like through the phone. I can't formulate words from my jumbled thoughts. So I just listen.

"Please, let me know if I can help in any way, but you should go to the police. Good luck, Ms. Hayes." The line goes dead, and an eerie stillness hangs low.

I scroll through the pictures in Bill's text, vacillating between being hopeful that this is all a big mistake and feeling shattered by what I already know to be true. The teal-blue house stands composed. Taunting. The lawn is littered with cardboard boxes, a face-down television, a white pail, a broom, and an old motorcycle. It is all too inconceivable to digest.

Did he devise this plan a year-and-a-half ago when we met? Was this always the end-game? Was I being primed and prepped all this time? I can't even fathom that, because our love was so full and rich.

I keep scrolling, reality slowly seeping in. There is no garden. There is no house. There was never a garden. There was never a house. That spring morning when we walked hand-in-hand, from floor to floor while I looked lovingly into his eyes, I was blissfully unaware that the wool was carefully and elaborately being pulled over mine. The small fragment of hope that I nursed in my chest unravels as I hobble on crutches around my apartment, the pain in my foot intensifying. I scan the memories of a love affair that was only real to me. The candlelight dinners on the glass-top table overlooking the East River, the recliner in which he napped, his slippers, his boots, his toothbrush, and his side of the bed.

My hands are trembling as I lift them to stifle a scream, a burning rage making its way through my body. I snatch his boxers, tee shirts and socks from the drawer and toss them in the hallway leading to the front door. Then I add his hairbrush and toothbrush to the pile. I limp to the kitchen, fling the cabinets open and yank his shaker cup and container of protein powder from the shelf and toss it on the growing pile. I hobble to the bedroom and pull his dirty laundry from the basket. It's tough to move about on crutches, but I make several wobbly trips to the incinerator and pour all his stuff through the square opening, listening as they tumble and fall to the fiery bottom.

I flop down on the couch. I feel as if I am being suffocated. Two cups of chamomile tea and a pile of used tissues later, I read and re-read his texts, my responses, his silly selfies, countless love emojis and sweet nothings of love. I cringe at the memories that are etched in my phone. Still too sacred to delete.

I lie in my bed for the next six days with the room-darkening curtains that he installed, drawn, my mind bending in the darkest sadness I have ever felt. Grieving for what I thought we had. Who I believed he was.

On the seventh day, I grab my iPad and reactivate my subscription to the dating website where we met, looking for him, but hoping not to find him. I search for him among a sea of shiny smiles and colorful faces. I scroll through pages and pages of photos and wordy profiles, still hoping that this is a wild colossal misunderstanding.

His lips are turned upward into a wide smile. Beads of sweat and cold chills compete for my skin as he stares back at me from behind the screen of my iPad. A jagged breath escapes me as I read his profile. He now goes by the name of Israel P.

His young son stands behind him in his profile picture. I zoom in and study each detail. Some of the pictures were taken in my building, and in one, he is boldly wearing my white long- sleeved running shirt. I feel weak. He lists himself as an accountant and a college graduate. Both lies.

In the A Little about Me section: "I pride myself in having taken care of myself all my life. I have a great sense of humor and I love the company of a woman who loves God more than me." In the One I'm Looking for section: "Looking for someone who can appreciate a man's transition from bad boy to a real man."

I write a letter to the e-mail address reserved for complaints on the Our Time website. I report an ex-convict with the profile name of Israel P. A man who uses their dating sites for the sole purpose of trolling for his next scam victims. I describe my shocking experience with this person, whose real name is Javier De Leon from the Mount Hope section of the Bronx. I send screenshots of all his pictures and his fabricated profile. I urge them to investigate and ban him from their site.

The thought of another woman enduring such pain leaves me shaken.

Two hours later they respond and thank me for reporting Israel P. They inform me that although they are unable to disclose what specific action has been taken, I should rest assured that the matter has been addressed. I am beyond overwhelmed.

I dig around in my purse until I find the business card

with the information for my company's Employee Assistance Program that provides 24-hour counseling services to our employees and dial the toll-free number.

"Good evening, this is Maryann, with whom am I speaking?"

"Hi Maryann, this is Donna." I am already crying.

"Donna, before we proceed, I need to ask you a few questions and I need to record your responses. Is that okay?" Maryann's voice is soothing.

"Yes."

"Are you in danger of hurting yourself?"

"No."

"Are you in danger of hurting someone else?"

"No."

"Do you understand that our conversation is being recorded and is strictly confidential, except if you are entertaining thoughts of hurting yourself and/or someone else?"

"I do."

"So, what is the purpose of your call tonight?"

For the next hour, I whimper and stutter while telling Maryann my story. The crying comes in waves with moments of short pauses and jagged breathing, before starting a new set of dry racking sobs. I want to stop crying. But I can't shut it off.

This continues nightly for the next three weeks. Each night a different counselor holds the space for me in silence as I rock back and forth on the bedroom floor. Some just listen until I am cried out, too spent to keep talking. Others point out my strengths, successes, and accomplishments. A few take the "This too shall pass" approach.

Until the Tuesday night when Priscilla answers. She listens for a while before interrupting my wailing mid-stream.

"Donna. It's just money and you can make more. He can't." Her candor shocks me. "Imagine his miserable existence if the only way he can earn a living is to steal! You are a good person with a good heart. He is not worthy of your tears. Count yourself lucky that a demented, convicted criminal with bad intentions did not kill you to conceal his crime. This man carved your initials in his chest to give you a false sense of security, so that he can do what he does best, steal. You made a mistake. So what? We all want to believe that people are inherently decent.

You got a bad one, just throw him back on the pile. Don't give him any of your power and be gentle with yourself. Rest assured that one day he will implode into a million pieces of bad decisions. You can't go back and not believe him. You can't go back and not give him money. You can't go back. So, you must find a way to move forward. Please don't let him break you."

I slowly unfurl after our call ended, her words buzzing in my ears, shaking me from my trance.

Please don't let him break you. Be gentle with yourself.
Don't give him any of your power.

I unclench my mind and allow her words to circulate in my brain.

Three months later, on a cold Thursday afternoon, I walk through the Manhattan precinct doors. I am not sure what to expect. Maybe something akin to a scene from *Law and Order,* complete with a flurry of activity including a host of handcuffed and irate criminals. Streetwalkers. Men sleeping it off behind thick vertical black bars. None of that is happening. The officer at the tall wooden desk in the center of the waiting area looks up as I enter. He motions for me to take a seat on the long wooden bench and turns his attention back to a woman draped in pearls cradling a poodle. He takes notes. She speaks quietly.

To my left is a small glass office in which a female officer is typing and talking on a cell phone. A large white board is sprawled on the wall above her. To my right is a circular silver-framed clock that I have glanced at, at least three times since entering. I need Poodle Lady to hurry up. Tension and anxiety are building up in me. I feel fidgety and nervous on this long wooden bench, mortified because of the circumstances that led me here. I think of the only other time I had reason to speak to a police officer. The day the constable walked into the yard after Naomi concocted the story that I had pushed her in front of the car. Betrayal. A recurring theme.

I place my hands on my knees and take deep breaths, trying to push the unease that is trying to crawl up my throat. Fifteen minutes later Poodle Lady exits, and the officer beckons for me to approach.

"How may I help you?" The desk officer with thick brown hair and brown eyes studies me from behind gunmetal-colored spectacles.

"I would like to file a police report." I try to breathe calmly.

"Okay. What about?" He is studying my face.

"A robbery?" I clasp and unclasp my hands.

"Was it your property?"

"Yes, it was."

He writes the date at the top of an official–looking pad, before taking my name, address, and contact information. "Okay. Tell me what happened." He seems bored and I suspect that this is very routine for him.

"My ex-con ex-boyfriend stole almost $200,000 from me." I can read the shock in his bright brown eyes.

"Did you say $200,000?"

"It's $162,000, to be exact," I punt back.

"Go on?" His pen moves across the page.

"He conned me into buying his cousin's house, which was never for sale. I emptied my bank account, took out a loan and borrowed from my pension, believing that I was buying my retirement property." I take a deep breath trying not to get emotional, before continuing. "He disappeared with my money and left me with loans. Not to mention that he is back on the dating website with a profile of lies, trying to trick his next victim. He already has a criminal record and should go back to jail—"

I realize that he has stopped writing. My eyes dart from the pad to his face and back to the pad. Why isn't he writing?

"Did you give him the money freely?"

"Yes, to give to his cousin and the contractor," I blubber. Confused.

"That is called Theft by Deception. He conned you. That sort of crime is on the rise, especially on the Upper East Side. We could go after him if he broke into your home and stole it, but not if he conned you."

So it's the method that he used to steal, not the theft itself. His words are like a sledgehammer against my head.

"Well, he did not break into my home and steal it, but he stole it nevertheless." I stare at him, my insides pleading as I try to ignore the tears that are crawling down my face.

"There are services that we provide, if you need someone to talk to, but this is a civil matter." He hands me a card with a weak smile.

I stop listening and stare at the gray-tiled floor. A sick feeling of disappointment leaves me weak as I try to process what I just heard. There is nothing that he can do to help me. Javier will not be arrested. He is going to get away with it! I want to scream, but instead I take a deep breath before looking up at the officer.

"So, what are my options?" I ask, trying to stop my hands from shaking.

"Your options are reporting him to the FBI, DA, the FTC and/or file a lawsuit," he says matter-of-factly.

I stand in front of him for what seemed like minutes trying to process his disappointing response. "Thank you for your help, officer." I wipe my face and take the card.

"Good luck, Ms. Hayes."

"Thank you."

The brisk wind tickles my face as I exit the precinct and fall in line with the rush-hour crowd. Time stands still and I feel an inner shift taking place within me as I move along the Manhattan sidewalks. If they can't help me, I will have to help myself.

I don't want to carry the burden of anger and regret anymore. I don't want to be ashamed, and I vehemently denounce the idea of being a victim. My inner fighter is stirring. I am ready to be released from the miserable patterns of giving people passes at my expense. Empath no more.

"I will not be your victim, Javier De Leon," I whisper to nobody. "I will not be your victim."

I hire a New York lawyer and sue Javier De Leon and his cousin for theft and fraud.

Like my visit to the precinct, this is a first for me. As a Wall Street human resources professional, I have had ample exposure to litigation, but when you are personally invested, it is markedly more stressful and riddled with angst. Not to mention the cost. The process becomes an all-consuming second job and I find it hard to focus on anything else. I collect evidence, prepare copious notes, respond to interrogatories, prepare for depositions, and sign off on statements.

Almost five months to the day after I watched him disappear behind the midtown Hilton Hotel with my life savings, I file a lawsuit in The Supreme Court of the State of New York.

Panic attacks and my exaggerated startle response syndrome, often associated with PTSD, are heightened. I am forced to relive details that I would much rather forget as I assemble text messages, photographs and video footage. Opposing counsel is as adversarial and aggressive as they come. I make peace with my dilemma and prepare myself for the long journey.

I call the FBI's office and an agent who uses a number to identify himself instead of a name takes my personal information. Never in a million years would I have imagined that I would have a reason to contact the Federal Bureau of Investigation. The agent sounds formal and serious when he asks me to explain what happened. The words gush out of me. I listen to him typing as I tell my story about how I met Javier De Leon, where he lives, his delivery job at PostMates, his prior conviction, the house in Connecticut, the scam and the theft. I get it all out, leaving my throat dry.

Yet it's freeing. Empowering. The agent thanks me for contacting the FBI and asks me to file the complaint on the FBI's website using the form IC3. I do. I also make reports to the FTC, IRS, Medicaid and the District Attorney's office. I put the sordid details of my sixteen-month relationship with a con artist out on the world wide web for all with an internet connection to see. His identity and his wickedness forever memorialized in the annals of New York's court system. I do this for me and for all the women who may cross his path, broken, vulnerable and trusting. Unaware of the extent of his degeneracy.

I sit on the floor and rip open the large official-looking envelope from my lawyer's office. I study the thick pile of legal documents. The Summons and Complaint, the exhibits, and the Affirmation/Affidavit of Service. The last document catches my attention. I study the report closely.

The process server entered Javier's building on The Grand Concourse on October 28, 2017, at 1:44 p.m. A Latina woman who appeared to be in her seventies opened the door. She stood approximately 5'1" tall, with black hair and tan skinned. She confirmed that Javier De Leon lives there with her in the tenth floor apartment but was not at home. She was asked whether Javier is in the military service of the State of New York or the United States. She confirmed that he was not. The process server asks her to confirm her relationship to Javier. She identified herself as his mother.

The mother who suffered from emphysema and was dying. The mother who died on a cool Thursday morning. The mother whose wake and funeral her son needed time and space to plan is alive and well.

A chill runs up my spine. I shudder to think of the extent that this man went to, to deceive me. I grab my phone and stare at the picture of the body in the coffin that he sent me on the day of her "wake." I zoom in on the picture and wonder who is in the coffin.

Sophia is standing at the customer service desk when I enter the branch. She sees me and waves me over excitedly.

"Hey, lady! So how is the house? Where are my pictures?"

The wide smile on her face makes my heart sink. I close my eyes and take deep breaths. The tears escape.

"What happened?" She beckons for someone to relieve her and steps from behind the desk and ushers me to one of the cubicles. I don't want to talk about it, and I am tired of crying about it.

"It was all a lie, Sophia. There was no house. My boyfriend scammed me," I whisper.

"He stole all that money?" Her eyes are as wide as saucers.

"He took the money and disappeared. He told me that his mother died and that he needed time to grieve, so that he could distance himself from me. But she is not dead." I sniff.

"He called down death on his own mother over money. What a vile piece of shit!"

"Yup!" I nod and smile weakly at her.

"You listen to me! Karma is a wild crazy bitch. Plus, there is a God in Heaven that sits high and looks low. You will be okay. He is going to get his. Cause that money is going to eat him alive!" Sophia wraps her arms around me as customers look on. "Wipe your eyes and leave it all in the hands of the good Lord. He will take you through." She pulls a tissue from a Kleenex box on the desk and hands it to me.

"My grandmother used to say things like that." I smile at her and give her one final hug. "Stop by and let me know how you are doing whenever you come into the branch, okay?"

"Okay," I reply with a grin.

"Promise?"

"Promise."

Nineteen

ABOVE THE FALLS

"FLIGHT ATTENDANTS, PLEASE PREPARE the cabin for landing." The captain's voice echoes over the intercom as the crew makes one last stroll down the aisle, scanning each row for trash. Seated in the first-class cabin of the American Airlines aircraft, my insides bubble in anticipation and excitement as I stare out the window at the island below. The plane pivots and dips toward Jamaica, the land of my birth.

I watch as our luggage is hurled into the back of a minivan. My older sister Grace, her son, my daughter and I take our seats, eager to start our vacation at the all-inclusive resort. I look around at the countryside, and then impatiently at our driver who is taking the last puffs from his cigarette. He flicks the tiny cigarette butt to the ground, smothers it with his boot, steps inside and sparks the engine to life. We meander through the idyllic countryside. Everything seems familiar, yet foreign, as I take in the landscape that stretches before us. We whiz past trees, farmhouses, pastures, rolling hills and people going about their day.

We enter Duncans, Trelawny, and a lump fills my throat. It has been forty-one years since I left this small town where I spent the first fourteen years of my life. A tsunami of childhood memories washes over me as we drive past the cemetery that used to terrify me, where Mama and Dada now rest together. The primary school where I was knocked down during recess. The corner where Naomi and I said goodbye for the last time before she was hit by a car. The road where we boarded a van with a nervous chicken. Tears come as I drive past my childhood.

About two hours later, we pull into a winding asphalt driveway with wide strips of green foliage on both sides of a glorious entrance. Giant floral arrangements in varying shades of orange, red and green lean against towering stone pillars. We exit the van and enter the hotel lobby. The bellhop unloads our luggage and beckons for us to follow him to the front desk. The tan-colored floors glisten like well-polished glass. I look around at the spacious grounds, beachside restaurants, a pristine beach, a beautiful coastal setting and one of the largest pools in the Caribbean. A far cry from the humble lifestyle of my childhood in Jamaica.

We drop our luggage and survey our suite with excitement. Luxurious king-sized beds, marbled floors, a sprawling leather sofa in the sitting area, waterfall power showers and a breathtaking view of the Caribbean Sea from our private terrace. We settle in for a week's vacation of zip-lining, bobsledding, relaxing on the pristine beaches, and the excursion I am mostly looking forward to, to Dunns River Falls.

I think back to the day of the Westwood class trip to Dunns River Falls when I was twelve years old. I wore the eggshell-colored two-piece bathing suit with scalloped edges that my mother bought for me. I remember gawking at the forceful gushing water, awestruck by its magnificence and decided that fairies and other magical creatures must live there. My schoolmates and I walked along the fringe of the waterfall, giggling, and chattering as the cool mist caressed our faces. Young hands formed a human chain and we slipped and squealed our way to the top. Then hurried back down and climbed up again and again and again, until it was time to return to school. That trip is one of my favorite childhood memories.

Frolicking at the waterfall that day stayed with me throughout my life. It was much more than child's play. It was a day that gave me a glimpse of how it felt to belong. I held hands with the pretty girls, the rich girls, and the popular girls and none of that mattered as we climbed the falls. It didn't matter that I didn't really know my mother or my father, or that my best friend had betrayed me, or that I felt abandoned like a stray dog most of my young life. I didn't have to try harder or do anything special to feel loved. We were all the same under the powerful waterfall.

Forty-one years later, I stand at the bottom of Dunns River Falls and stare with the same sense of wonder and childlike fascination that I felt on that class outing. Rays of sunlight puncture the canopy of trees above me as I prepare for the climb up the giant slippery nature-made stairs. Nostalgia mixed with painful memories suddenly rush to the surface. I think of Naomi and the day she got hit by the car. The day Sherlock and my sisters left. I think of my sweet Mama. The red veranda. My husbands. Javier De Leon.

With my arms linked with strangers, I begin my ascent, a mini pilgrimage of healing up the majestic Dunns River Falls. It is just as uneven and slippery as it was decades earlier. The water is forceful and relentless, and at times we break the link to grab large rocks for support against a deluge; to help someone who is scared or struggling; or get on all fours to steady ourselves. We become a community of strangers helping strangers. With each lingering step, I inhale peaceful breaths and focus on the sweet symphony of the waterfall. I pray and ask God to teach me how to forgive—not only others, but myself.

We get to the half-way point and a woman who has been holding my hand is overcome by fear and exhaustion. She moves through the opening at the half-way point, winded and gasping. I see my daughter ahead of me, holding the hand of a little boy. My nephew is helping his mom, my older sister, Grace. I reach for another hand and continue climbing, pushing against the powerful surges of water, clinging and clamoring. With each step, my emotions climb further up my throat and settle in my eyes. Despite all that has happened, I have so much to be grateful for, so I give thanks to the universe:

For the person I get to be each day. For the wonderful life that I get to live.

For all the painful lessons that I needed to learn, and for those I have yet to learn. For all the teachers who were disguised as bullies, husbands, parents and boyfriends. For successes that masqueraded as terrible failures.

For all the red verandas of my life that gave me comfort.

For the stories I have yet to write and the angels I have yet to meet. For my unique talents, flaws, traits, skills and fears.

For my good heart.

I reach the top, feeling a surge of inspiration and hope. I take in the sweeping view of droves of hand-holding tourists meandering under the shade of the lush green vegetation. The memory of that day on the class trip plays like another movie reel in my head, and I can almost see her.

Twelve-year-old me. Her two-piece eggshell-colored bathing suit with the scalloped edges moves among the wet bodies. She is giggling and pushing against the water. The lost young girl who yearned to belong, who was so desperate for her parents and their affection that she prayed to their pictures. The sensitive girl with the big heart who tried to save animals from getting slaughtered.

I wish I could go back in time to that sunny day in the 1970s and climb up these falls with my twelve-year self. To take her hand in mine. To stand with her. To whisper secrets that she will need to carry in her soul like a shield.

Donna,
You are stronger and braver than anything you will ever encounter. Never forget that the strength is in the stumble. It is in the fall. It is also in the getting back up. You will go through holy hell before you figure out who you really are and when you stopped being you. You are enough, Sweetheart; you have always been and always will be. You do not have to accept brokenness because it makes your brokenness feel less broken. Before you try to fix others, look inside, and make sure that you are not really trying to fix yourself. Keep Mama's words close to you because you are indeed special.

The sound of the powerful water pulls me from my reverie. I inhale deeply and give my pain and wounds to the powerful waterfall that rushes down to empty into the Caribbean Sea.

Four months later, a default judgment is entered against Javier De Leon for the full amount he stole. While I may never recover a dime, I feel a sense of vindication. For the first time in my life, I did not run. I stood. I fought. I felt empowered enough to step out from the corner of the red veranda of my youth to take my power back from all those who I handed it over to, by showing up diminished, hungry for love, but unconvinced of my worth, I settled for people who were nothing more than crumbs. I attracted and chose broken people as mates and set about to fix them in hopes that they would become the people that I desperately needed them to be.

As I propel myself forward, I have changed the narrative, and will continue to excavate the sludge of old wounds and change a lifetime of unhealthy patterns. Mama used to tell me that I am worthy, unique, and special. I choose to believe.

August 20, 2018

Dear Mama,

I went back home after forty-one years. I drove past the cemetery, and I know that you and Dada are resting in peace. I wish that I could have climbed that hill to the house to find you in your favorite spot, in the corner over the stove, cooking for us. I went to Dunns River Falls, and it was magical. I wish I could tell you about it.

Thank you for loving me and being like a mother to me. I have learned some very tough and painful lessons, Mama, but you used to tell me to leave it all in the hands of the Lord and he will guide my steps. I am still learning how to truly do that, Mama, and I believe that you would be proud of me as I work on being the best version of myself. I know that somewhere in heaven you and Dada are smiling down on me. Continue to rest in peace together. Until we meet again.

Your granddaughter,
Donna

EPILOGUE

TWO YEARS AFTER THE JAVIER DEBACLE, I decided to try online dating again.

Robert and I arranged to meet on a warm spring evening in 2019. I arrived early and waited for him by the host's station at Negril, a contemporary Jamaican restaurant in Greenwich Village. This was my first date after being scammed, and although I conducted a complete background check on him, I carried a sense of unease in my chest.

Familiar scents filled the air as servers, all dressed in white tunics, balanced platters teeming with stew peas and rice, curried chicken, yard food and the like. Aromas that never fail to transport me back to that tiny kitchen deep in the countryside of Jamaica, where Mama donned her patterned apron and hovered over the gas stove, her hands moving swiftly, as she grated, chopped and mixed ingredients in steaming pots. I am almost lost in the nostalgia of those sweet memories when Robert entered the restaurant.

We waved and smiled at each other as he climbed the stairs leading from the main entrance. After a hug and brief pleasantries, we followed our waiter to our table. We studied the menu before settling on codfish fritters as a shared appetizer.

I ordered my absolute favorite, ackee and saltfish with yard food and fried plantains. Robert opted for the oxtails entrée.

In the background, the restaurant was abuzz with activity, happy chatter and the clanging of silverware on plates, but in our little corner of the restaurant, Robert and I fell into a slow rhythm of steady conversation. I am laser-focused on his ruggedly handsome face, his salt-and- pepper locks that cascaded from beneath a tan baseball cap. Glinting eyes study me.

Guarded, I dissected every word and scrutinized every gesture, searching for something— anything—that would justify the creation of a fictitious reason to leave abruptly. I found nothing.

Robert is four years younger, but there is an undeniable alpha energy about him. But not in a bad way. A confident, protector, caretaker, defender kind of energy. We swapped stories about our childhoods, his in Mount Vernon, New York, and mine in Jamaica, West Indies. We share a love of God, Pentecostal church upbringing, a love of movies, animals and acting.

Conversely, he is a skilled driver; I find driving terrifying. I enjoy playing slot machines; he is averse to gambling. He loves house music. Show tunes for me. I have a corporate career. He has a background in law enforcement, EMT and drug testing. I love vegetables. Robert, not so much.

For two hours, we laughed, talked and listened with an ease that surprised me.

We left the restaurant and headed straight to the gas station, where he taught me how to pump gas, because I mentioned that I had never pumped gas before. Hilarity ensued. He drove me home to the soundtrack of house music blaring in his black Infiniti.

It has been four years, and he still insists on walking on the traffic side of the street and opening doors for me. We vacation, ride his motorcycle, frequent the theatre and experienced our first opera together. He threw me a 60th surprise birthday party at Negril—the restaurant of our first date—complete with all the foods that we enjoyed that beautiful spring evening. He has grown accustomed to me belting out random show tunes, and house music is beginning to grow on me. He is still not a fan of vegetables.

I have always believed that the best relationships are often when people are different, yet complementary, each bringing their unique qualities that enrich the life of the other. That is us.

Most importantly, we are mindful of each other's past and scars. We create a safe space for each other to feel what we feel, and do what we do. We are each other's cheerleaders and our soft place to fall.

I show up in this new relationship, renewed at my core, and brandish authenticity and self-worth.

Yet, I honor the younger me who tried to save animals from slaughter and pilfered crackers and jelly to be liked. A pattern woven into adult life choices with devastating results. As the architect of my own happiness, I have picked up the pieces, plucked the lessons from the wreckage and continue to move boldly and unapologetically in the direction of the amazing life that I deserve.

I don't know what the future holds, but I know that time has its own flow and agenda. So, I flow with it, passing time, soaking up new memories, and enjoying the quiet contentment that comes from knowing that I am finally done running.

I can be changed by what happens to me.
But I refuse to be reduced by it. – Maya Angelou

ACKNOWLEDGEMENTS

To my daughter Cierra, we walked side by side through some of these tear-stained pages. You gave me a purpose to keep going and a reason to fight back. Baby girl, you are my greatest gift.

To my sisters Janet and Cameale, thank you for traveling down memory lane with me to forage for forgotten childhood memories to enrich my story. I celebrate our sisterhood with this book.

To my parents, thank you for giving me life and the life experiences that have influenced my journey.

To Groovey, I love your incredible heart and appreciate your fierce support of all my endeavors, including getting this memoir published. Thank you for making me feel safe, honored and loved.

To my grandmother Mama, thank you for watching over me from heaven and for loving little girl Donna.

To my sister-friend Julie, you have been a remarkable source of support during all my undertakings, including scribing this memoir. A massive thank you to you and all my draft readers and loyal friends for honoring me with so much support.

I would like to express my deepest appreciation to my writing coach Joselin. Words are not sufficient to express my immense gratitude for your unwavering support, ingenious ideas, and expert counsel throughout this process.

Beth, your support over our four decades of friendship, especially during our younger years have left a profound imprint on my soul. Thank you for sharing what you had with me when I had nothing.

A special thank you to Sibylline Press and everyone on the publishing team for honoring my story with such care and reverence. I am thrilled to be a Sibyl.

To my former classmates at Gotham Writers, I am honored to have met each of you. Our mid-town Manhattan classroom where we sat in a semi-circle and read each other's stories was my weekly haven. A space in which it was ok to be vulnerable without judgement. Thank you for allowing me to share my truth and experience yours.

My childhood home in Jamaica

Mama, my grandmother who raised me

A letter I wrote at age 5 to my mother introducing myself. I assumed she had never met me because I was too young to remember her.

DONNA HAYES has been a senior human resource professional in the financial services industry for almost 30 years. Additionally, she is an ICF-certified coach and owner of a coaching practice company. When she is not wearing her corporate hat, she can be found on a stage or in front of a camera. Ms. Hayes is also a SAG-AFTRA actress and cabaret singer. She has been featured on the *Dr. Oz Show* (Defy Your Age), *Orange Is The New Black* (Netflix), *Black Girls Rock* (BET), *Celebrity Ghost Stories* (Biography Channel) as well as in several other New York City Off-Broadway and television productions. Most recently, she was cast in her first regular role in a TV series which is expected to debut soon. Finally, she is a mother of a daughter, a lifestyle model, certified Zumba Instructor and writer. *These Broken Roads* is Ms. Hayes' first memoir.

Enjoy more about
These Broken Roads
Meet the Author
Check out author appearances
Explore special features

BOOK GROUP QUESTIONS

For These Broken Roads by Donna Marie Hayes

1. How does Donna's relationship with her grandmother contrast with the relationship between Donna and her mother? Which relationship is the more valuable or important to young Donna?

2. Donna was left in Jamaica when her mother went to the United States, but she took some of her children with her. How would you decide which child to take and which child to leave behind with a grandmother?

3. Donna writes about the times she was saved by a miracle, being "protected" or "blessed." Which of these events was the most shocking or scary to you? What other events in this memoir felt like a blessing?

4. What role does religion play in some of the choices and events of Donna's life? What are some of the practices, beliefs or prayers that affected Donna's life?

5. How does Donna's self-esteem or self-love change through her life, and how does that make a difference in the outcome of her choices?

6. How does Donna's upbringing help ground her in the events that happen later in her life? How do her failures and successes reflect her experience as an immigrant or as a woman of color?

7. Donna's story can feel like a Cinderella story; talk about some of the ways that Donna lived a fairy tale life.

Sibylline Press is proud to publish the brilliant work of women authors over 50. We are a woman-owned publishing company and, like our authors, represent women of a certain age. In our first season we have three outstanding fiction (historical fiction and mystery) and three incredible memoirs to share with readers of all ages.

HISTORICAL FICTION

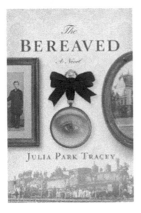

The Bereaved: A Novel
By Julia Park Tracey

Paperback ISBN: 978-1-7367954-2-2
5 3/8 x 8 3/4 | 274 pages | $18
ePub ISBN: 978-1-9605730-0-1 | $12.60

Based on the author's research into her grandfather's past as an adopted child, and the surprising discovery of his family of origin and how he came to be adopted, Julia Park Tracey has created a mesmerizing work of historical fiction illuminating the darkest side of the Orphan Train.

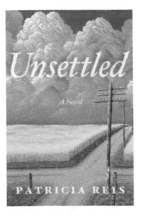

Unsettled: A Novel
By Patricia Reis

Paperback ISBN: 978-1-7367954-8-4
5 3/8 x 8 3/4 | 378 pages | $19
ePUB ISBN: 978-1-960573-05-6 | $13.30

In this lyrical historical fiction with alternating points of view, a repressed woman begins an ancestral quest through the prairies of Iowa, awakening family secrets and herself, while in the late 1800s, a repressed ancestor, Tante Kate, creates those secrets.

MYSTERY

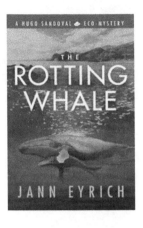

The Rotting Whale: A Hugo Sandoval Eco-Mystery
BY JANN EYRICH

Paperback ISBN: 978-1-7367954-3-9
5 3/8 x 8 3/8 | 212 pages | $17
ePub ISBN: 978-1-960573-03-2 | $11.90

In this first case in the new Hugo Sandoval Eco-Mystery series, an old-school San Francisco building inspector with his trademark Borsalino fedora, must reluctantly venture outside his beloved city and find his sea legs before he can solve the mystery of how a 90-ton blue whale became stranded, twice, in a remote inlet off the North Coast.

MORE TITLES IN THIS ECO-MYSTERY SERIES TO COME:
Spring '24: *The Blind Key* | ISBN: 978-1-7367954-5-3
Spring '25: *The Singing Lighthouse* | ISBN: 978-1-7367954-6-0

MEMOIR

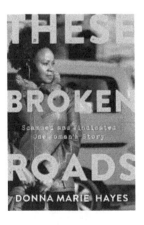

These Broken Roads: Scammed and Vindicated, One Woman's Story
BY DONNA MARIE HAYES

Tradepaper ISBN: 978-1-7367954-4-6
5 3/8 x 8 3/8 | 226 pages | $17
ePUB ISBN: 978-1-960573-04-9 | $11.90

In this gripping and honest memoir, Jamaican immigrant Donna Marie Hayes recounts how at the peak of her American success in New York City, she is scammed and robbed of her life's savings by the "love of her life" met on an online dating site and how she vindicates herself to overcome a lifetime of bad choices.

Maeve Rising: Coming Out Trans in Corporate America
By MAEVE DUVALLY

Paperback ISBN: 978-1-7367954-1-5
5 3/8 x 8 3/8 | 284 pages | $18
ePub ISBN: 978-1-960573-01-8 | $12.60

In this searingly honest LBGQT+ memoir, Maeve DuVally tells the story of coming out transgender in one of the most high-profile financial institutions in America, Goldman Sachs.

Reading Jane: A Daughter's Memoir
By SUSANNAH KENNEDY

Paperback ISBN: 978-1-7367954-7-7
5 3/8 x 8 3/8 | 306 pages | $19
ePub ISBN: 978-1-960573-02-5 | $13.30

After the calculated suicide of her domineering and narcissistic mother, Susannah Kennedy grapples with the ties between mothers and daughters and the choices parents make in this gripping memoir that shows what freedom looks like when we choose to examine the uncomfortable past.

Sibylline
PRESS

For more information about Sibylline Press and our authors, please visit us at **www.sibyllinepress.com**